Political Skills at Workplace

FIZZA RIZVI

Abstract

The emphasis of this research dissertation is to investigate political skill and its outcomes at different levels, i.e. employee level outcomes and supervisor level outcome. Political skill has been attracting immense research attention in recent years. Majority of the researches showed positive outcomes of political skill for employees. This research will provide new insights to the literature through investigating the role of political skill in reducing the negative behavioral outcomes of the employees by developing job satisfaction to ultimately reduce turnover intention. Moreover, the harmonizing effect of political skill in perceived organizational politics may enable employees to maintain job satisfaction and reduce turnover intention. To extend the scope of study, the impact of political skill has been investigated at supervisor level outcome as well. An important supervisor level behavior of perceived abusive supervision is explored in this research. Abusive supervision in organizations is becoming a dominant phenomenon that is also gaining more research attention. Numerous supervisor and subordinate related factors have been investigated as the antecedents and outcomes of the phenomenon. The current research investigates if employees possessing good political skill face less abusive behavior of the supervisor. Moreover, the moderating role of the gender of the subordinate is tested with the earlier relationship. The study indicates an inverse relation of political skill and abusive supervision. Furthermore, male subordinates use political skill more proficiently to avoid abusive supervision. The study is undertaken in a developing country which provides relevant conditions to investigate such a relationship. The data are collected from private organizations. These studies add to the literature in the fields of political skill, organizational politics and abusive supervision.

Dedication

Dedicated to

My Parents, Husband and Son

Table of Contents

List of Figures

List of Tables

List of Abbreviations

Symbol	Abbreviation
AVE	Average Variance Extracted
CFA	Confirmatory Factor Analysis
CFI	Comparative Fit Index
GFI	Goodness of Fit Index
RMSEA	Root Mean Square Error of Approximation
AMOS	Analysis of Moment Structures
SPSS	Statistical Package for the Social Sciences
CMV	Common Method Variance Bias
SRMR	Standardized Root Mean Square Residual
TLI	Tucker-Lewis Index

Chapter 1

Introduction

The primary focus of this research dissertation is on political skill as a resource to cope with the workplace stressors at different levels such as employee level and supervisor level. Numerous studies have acknowledged the significant negative outcomes of two important workplace stressors i.e. perceived organizational politics and abusive supervision. In this research, organizational factor like perceived organizational politics is studied for the impact on employee outcomes. The study tests the indirect impact of employee political skill on turnover intention through job satisfaction as a coping mechanism to reduce the negative impact of perceived organizational politics. Such that it investigates the role of perceived organizational politics on the relationship of political skill and job satisfaction, and further, on turnover intention. To examine the impact of supervisor level stressor, the study tests the impact of employee political skill on abusive supervision and the moderating role of employee gender on the established relationship. These studies serve by adding to the existing literature in the field of organizational politics, political skill and abusive supervision.

Earlier research on organizational politics has focused majorly on politics within the organization (Ferris et al. 2005). This has been the main focus of researchers since the perception about the existence of such an environmental factor was interesting and a potential area for improvement in different ways. However, the influence exerted by individuals with better political know-how (later referred to as political skill) started gaining attention during the same time (e.g. Mintzberg 1983; Pfeffer 1981). Since politics in organizations was mainly influencing the people working there, investigating about traits or skills helping them to cope with such situations was considered imperative. Pfeffer (1981) in his research, considered politics and political skill as a primary source of acquiring power. Though an initial idea about the skill set required for achieving positive outcomes in organizations was proposed, Pfeffer (1981) highlighted the need of additional exploration in the field of political skill.

1.1 Political Skill

Modern day organizational settings are finely knitted and socially constructed. The success of the people within the organizations does not depend solely on the expertise and the technical knowledge they possess or have acquired through academia. It is also highly dependent on different social, personal and situational attributes (Luthans, Hodgetts and Rosenkrantz 1988). Merely learned knowledge is not enough to get ahead on the career path; in fact, knowledge about dealing with people and responding to different situations is one of the prime skills to enable success in professional life. The progressively more social and unclear nature of work has elevated the importance of being able to recognize and explore the social fabric of organizations (Grant et al. 2010). Recognizing the importance of these traits and skills, this dissertation takes employee political skill (PS) as a vital personal skill to be focused on for in-depth research. Though the research on politics and political skill has covered a wide range of theoretical and practical areas, there are few noticeable gaps in the literature. Presently, the prime focus of political skill (PS) research had been on its outcomes and buffering effects as moderator. Not only does the research establish that political skill results in positive outcomes, but it also proves that some negative situational and personal outcomes can be marginally reduced by those employees possessing political skill.

Research in the field of politics has indicated the need for more intense focus on organizational politics (Gandz and Murray 1980). Theoretically, politics intervenes in the usual functions of an organization and impacts performance at both the individual and organizational level (Vigoda 2000). Knowing the potential effect of politics in the organization, its importance should not be underestimated (Vigoda 2000). However, the literature suggests that an individual's perception of events actually creates their reality (Lewin 1936). Therefore, perception of politics rather than actual politics affects various workplace outcomes (Ferris, Russ and Fandt 1989; Gandz and Murray 1980). The literature on perceived organizational politics has shown varied evidence concerning its outcomes, yet an overarching understanding considers its detrimental effect on the organizational members and job outcomes (Abbas and Raja 2014). However, Brouer, Harris and Kacmar (2011) have argued that given different personality traits and skills of employees, perceived organizational politics may have unalike influence on the work outcomes. This dissertation takes a similar stance, where politically skilled individuals consider the organizational environment as a level playing field due to their perception of high politics in the organization. Politically skilled employees can be poor at their jobs, but nevertheless will succeed in the organization because of their political skill. It is argued that such individuals may not show undesirable workplace outcomes due to their shrewdness. Predominantly there is lack of literature on perceived organizational politics from this perspective.

Advancing the research in the direction that PS may reduce the negative impact of workplace stressor, another harmful stressor, abusive supervision, will be studied. Previous research has focused on various detrimental workplace behaviors (Tepper 2007); however, organizations these days are facing numerous adverse outcomes due to the prevalence of abusive supervision. Initially presented by Tepper (2000), abusive supervision refers to the display of a supervisor's hostile behavior towards subordinates. To talk about the practical implications of the phenomenon, 14% of the workforce in the USA is affected by abusive supervision (Kelloway, Barling and Hurrell 2006) causing a huge financial impact (Tepper et al. 2006). Since the detrimental impacts of abusive supervision are fairly acknowledged in the literature, research must focus attention on what is required to potentially avoid it. A vast literature has suggested that the antecedent of abusive supervision (AS) is predominantly supervisor related meaning thereby generally supervisors' personal traits and personalities evoke abusive behavior by them (Mawritz et al. 2012; Liu, Liao and Loi 2012; Kiewitz et al. 2012, Tepper, Simon and Park 2017). However, the recent streams of study also focus on subordinate related behaviors, skills and traits that trigger abusive behavior of the supervisors (Khan et al. 2016; Liang et al. 2016; Wang et al. 2016). Most researchers have discussed the personal attributions that cause change in the perception about abusive supervision, such as the fact that positive affectivity ameliorates the impact of abusive supervision (Harvey et al. 2007a), and subordinates with high core self-evaluations perceive less abusive supervision (Wu and Hu 2009). However, these attributions cannot be learnt socially. Though theoretically many factors have been identified which pacify abusive supervision, not all of them can be learned or adopted by everyone in general. Research in skills and traits that can be socially learnt and exercised to avoid abusive behavior is scarce. This research proposed PS as an antecedent that reduced the abusive behavior of supervisors.

In the literature, political skill has been considered to be an important resource for workers (Ferris et al. 2005; Pfeffer 1981; Mintzberg 1983). Though extensive research has proved various constructive outcomes of this skill (Bing et al. 2011; Munyon et al. 2015; Treadway et al. 2007; Maher et al. 2018), the current study takes into account a dual level of the constructive outcomes of political skill (PS) i.e. it pacifies the negative outcomes on two levels. The research at employee level outcomes investigated whether the politically skilled employees have better job satisfaction levels which result in lower turnover intention. Moreover, the impact of perceived organizational politics (POP) and political skill (PS) on the outcomes was investigated in a different cultural setting. At a supervisor level, the study tested whether political skill helps in reducing the abusive behavior of the supervisors. This study discusses political skill as a potential buffer against abusive supervision. The most significant contribution of this study is that, since political skill is a social skill, employees can learn it to avoid harmful workplace behaviors. Further, this study also examines the moderating role of gender to explore the difference in the utilization and outcomes of political skill among males and females.

1.2 Political Skill, Organizational Politics and its Outcomes

The importance of understanding the social fabric of a given organization has significantly increased as modern-day organizations have become more complex and intensely socially interwoven (Grant et al. 2010). Many factors influence the workflow of the organizations. Hence, to effectively influence and maintain work relationships, various skills, traits and qualities are expected from the employees. Examining the political aspects of organizations, earlier research has highlighted the need for certain personal attributes including personal savvy or shrewdness to ensure success (Pfeffer 1981). To sustain such environmental factors, political skill (PS) – "the ability to effectively understand others at work, and to use such knowledge to influence others to act in ways that enhance one's personal and/or organizational objectives" (Ferris et al. 2005 pg. 127) – can play a critical role (Munyon et al. 2015). Political skill has been established as a function of four dimensions including social astuteness, interpersonal influence, networking ability and apparent sincerity (Ferris et al. 2007), all of which help to develop better social connections.

Recent research results from studies in political skill suggest it to be crucial in producing positive organizational outcomes (Ferris et al. 2012). Munyon et al. (2015) have discussed the significantly positive relationship between PS and performance. Employees having good political skill are also better in positive impression management (Treadway et al. 2007). PS has also been associated with positive social life quality (Wang and Hall 2019). In a recent study, PS has also been linked with adaptive selling behavior of the salesperson (Kimura, Bande and Fernández-Ferrín 2019).

Political skill has also been investigated in its role as a buffer between harmful situational or behavioral issues. This role suggests that not only does it produce positive outcomes for organizations, but it also helps to reduce potentially negative outcomes (Zhou et al., 2015). PS has been used as a personal resource to deal with stressful situations in the workplace (Karatepe, Kim and Lee 2019). In another study, political skill has been postulated as a way to reduce the negative effects of workplace ostracism (Zhao, Peng and Sheard 2013). Politically skilled individuals are better able to work in uncertain conditions (Kacmar et al. 2013). Jawahar, Stone and Kisamore (2007) demonstrated negative correlation between political skill and emotional exhaustion.

In organizational behavior literature, job satisfaction (JS) and turnover intention (TI) have been considered very significant behavioral outcomes of employees because of their significant impact on job performance. Primarily, job satisfaction is significant as it depicts the subjective evaluation of the working conditions of the organization (Dormann and Zapf 2001) which includes responsibility, variety of tasks, or communication requirements (Hackman and Oldham 1980) all of which are considered as predictors of job satisfaction (Dormann and Zapf 2001). Moreover, it is imperative to take into account the level of job satisfaction (JS) of the workers, as mostly negative work outcomes are dependent on the satisfaction levels (Dormann and Zapf 2001). Turnover intention also has a significantly negative impact on organizations due to the cost of hiring new employees and the loss of former employees. Considering the importance of these important organizational outcomes, the present study focused on them as dependent variables. Since the positive effects of job satisfaction and adverse effects of turnover intention are well understood, the factors influencing these outcomes also need in-depth attention. The present study, however, addresses the impact of the personal factor, i.e. political skill, on job satisfaction and turnover intention.

Additionally, employee level outcomes have tremendous practical significance. Considering the importance of PS of employees to organizations and the scarce number of studies investigating the subordinate related outcomes, the current research model focuses on investigating the relationship of PS to both Job Satisfaction (JS) and Turnover Intentions (TI), since human resources are the primary asset of an organization (Jyoti and Rani 2019). Organizations are becoming more competitive for employee retention (Korsakienė et al. 2015), and therefore, factors that ensure employee retention should be comprehensively covered in the literature. PS has been investigated as a predictor of job satisfaction and turnover intention.

Literature suggests that the perception of the reality, rather than reality itself, forms the behavioral outcomes of individuals (Lewin 1936). Practically, whatever surrounds us is nothing but what we perceive it to be, whether it is a material object or behavior, emotion, attitude or situation. The response of an individual depends upon how he or she observes the surroundings. The research has objectified the impact of perceptions by examining the interplay of Perceived Organizational Politics (POP) and political skill. Perceived organizational politics (POP) denotes the individual's perception of the political environment of the organization, which, "involves an individual's attribution to behaviors of self-serving intent, and is defined as an individual's subjective evaluation about the extent to which the work environment is characterized by coworkers and supervisors who demonstrate such self-serving behavior" (Ferris, Harrell-Cook and Dulebohn 2000, p. 90). Therefore, the perception of politics (POP) in an organization may not be the same for all employees, since people can perceive the environment differently. Ferris and Kacmar (1992) have argued that the perception of employees regarding organizational politics, rather than actual politics prevailing in the organization, defines and influences different reactions and responses of the individuals. Perceived organizational politics has been negatively related to job satisfaction whereas positively related to turnover intention (Labrague et al. 2017)

Therefore, grounded on the foundation provided by the literature on the difference of actual and perceived politics, the present study investigated the moderating role of POP in determining the effect of political skill on job satisfaction. More specifically, the study investigated how the perception of organizational politics of a politically skilled individual affects the level of job satisfaction. The motivating question concerned whether the politically skilled employees exploit the organizational politics in their favor to achieve higher levels of job satisfaction, or whether they just remain indifferent to the political arenas around them.

A number of research studies have examined the moderating effects of organizational elements, such as justice and political climate, on the relationship between PS and job outcomes, but with contradictory or insignificant findings (Brouer et al. 2011; Haider, Fatima and Pablos-Heredero 2020; Kimura 2015), thus calling for additional investigation. Though different contexts and cultures impact the hypothesized relationships, surprisingly there is a gap in the literature that needs to be addressed comprehensively. The reason for taking POP as a moderating variable here is to keep two aspects of politics together for the purpose of establishing an interconnection between them.

Current empirical evidence suggests a positive relationship between PS and JS (Munyon et al. 2015: Meisler 2014). But no research that extends this link to turnover intention has been found. This research gap is surprising as JS is a strong predictor of TI (Fasbender, Van der Heijden and Grimshaw 2019). The current study presents some new insights while exploring the link between PS and employee perception of politics (POP). Furthermore, the research model has been extended to test the ultimate impact of the relationship on employee turnover intention, which is an underexplored area in the PS literature. Private sector organizations have been selected from Pakistan (a developing country) for collecting the data in the current study. Pakistan is a suitable cultural setting for research on organizational politics due to inherent power distant, collectivistic and uncertainty avoidance settings, providing an ideal situation for investigating the model developed (Naseer et al. 2016). This research will advance our understanding of how PS contributes to workplace outcomes such as job satisfaction (JS) and turnover intention (TI), which are the key organizational factors.

1.3   Political Skill and Abusive Supervision

An increasing focus in organizational behavior research concerns the dark side of leadership. Specifically, research has been focusing on the negative practices and personalities of leaders and how they both affect the performance, attitudes and behaviors of the followers/ subordinates. A very prominent area of research these days is focusing on abusive supervision (Bennett et al. 2018) i.e. the "subordinates' perceptions of the extent to which supervisors engage in the sustained display of hostile verbal and nonverbal behaviors, excluding physical contact" (Tepper 2000, p. 178). Tepper (2007) has reported an increase in consumer cost due to the negative outcomes resulting from abusive supervision. Researchers are interested not only in the consequences of the practice (Han, Harms and Bai 2017; Liu et al. 2012), but also in the antecedents and provoking attitudes and behaviors manifested in abusive supervision (Brees et al. 2014; Khan et al. 2016; Tepper, Moss and Duffy 2011). Abusive supervision (AS) is considered to be a threatening issue in many organizations (Liang et al. 2016). Moreover, a number of organizational and individual effects are surfacing due to AS (Lian, Ferris and Brown 2012). AS has been associated to numerous detrimental effects comprising low levels of performance (Ayree, Chen and Budhwar 2007), reduced psychological well-being (Tepper 2007) and low job satisfaction and organizational commitment (Tepper 2000). Mitchell and Ambrose (2007) found supervisor-related deviance, organizational deviance, and interpersonal deviance as an outcome of AS. Further, it is counted as a workplace stressor (Haggard, Robert and Rose 2011). Recent literature explains low organizational citizenship behavior (OCB) and raised counter-productive work behavior (CWB) among employees because of abusive supervision (Zhang et al. 2019). Abusive supervision represents injustice as anticipated fair exchange is violated (Zhang et al. 2019), and hence is a threat to maintaining an ethical workplace environment (Ünal, Warren and Chen 2012). Moreover, organization support theory (Rhoades and Eisenberger 2002) explains adverse employee attitudes in response to AS.

Zhang and Bednall (2016), in their meta-analysis conducted on the antecedents of AS, presented four categories i.e. supervisor related, organization related, subordinate related and demographic characteristics of both supervisor and subordinate. Recently, Khan et al. (2017, p.166) noted that "most of these studies have been focused on the supervisors' characteristics and perceptions and far less is currently known about the potential roles played by subordinates' own characteristics or cognitions as antecedents of perceived abusive supervision." Furthermore, the research on gender differences related to abusive supervision is limited (Wang et al. 2016). As a response to these observations, the current study investigates a model including the subordinate related characteristic (political skill) and demographic characteristic (subordinate gender) in relation to abusive supervision. As discussed in the theoretical framework, the few empirical studies combining political skill and abusive supervision suggest contradictory relationships, calling for additional investigation.

Kernan and Watson (2011) highlighted the dearth of research on AS in different cultural settings as most of the research in this area has been done in American settings. An early review by Tepper (2007) suggested the prospect of investigating the phenomenon in non-American cultures. However, as cultural diversity in the organizations has increased and is not limited only to the organizational boundaries but also caters to outsourcing, the need to understand differences in the cultural values and attitudes has immensely increased (Kernan and Watson 2011). The supervisor and subordinate relationship is certainly an important work environment factor (Kernan and Watson 2011); however, this relation depends upon cultural values (Lawler, Walumbwa and Bai 2008). Since abusive supervision is as much a subjective assessment as it is a perception by definition (Tepper 2007), the culture influences the diverse assessments of this perception. Kernan and Watson (2011) explained that abusive supervision is the perception of injustice, and therefore, cultural values may impact the justice perception of the victim. Both the response and reaction of the subordinate, and also the antecedent of AS from different cultures explain the cause of an event as resulting from environmental (external attribution) or dispositional factors (internal attribution) (Heider 1958). Literature evidently acknowledges the difference while determining attributing factors among different cultures. Asians, for example, consider the situational factors more than do Americans (Lee, Hallahan and Herzog 1996). These differences provide a very strong base for conducting research on AS and its antecedents in an Asian setting. Moreover, Pakistan's high-power distance culture makes it a suitable setting for the prevalence of AS (Khan et al. 2016). Particularly with respect to gender differences, the contextual settings of Pakistan offer a very significant area of exploration. Gelfand et al. (2011) in their research identified Pakistan's culture as a tight culture, where societal norms are strongly held and any deviation in their execution may result in severe sanctions (Triandis, 1989). A recent study highlighted slightly successful outcomes of governmental attempts to bring at par both genders with respect to employment and equality (Ali and Syed, 2017). Strong contextual, sociocultural differences and lack of genuine commitment at the policy level, however, hinder any attempt to achieve gender equality at workplaces (Ali and Syed, 2017). Therefore, the present research will also explore the difference in supervisors' response towards both genders who possess good political skill.

Subordinate characteristics are observed to influence reactions towards abusive supervision (Tepper 2007). Within the domain of organizational behavior literature, social influence research explains how individuals deal with each other to gain the required outcomes (Ferris and Mitchell 1987). The literature related to this area has also increased and expanded (McAllister, Ellen III and Ferris 2016), as keen interest in this area by researchers dates back to over a century (Triplett 1898). One of the important areas of this domain covers politics in organizations. Politics in organizations has gained considerable attention since the 1960's in management studies (Kimura 2015) as a very important social influencer. Micro-politics has been observed in multinational organizations also (Sharpe 2006). Aryee et al. (2004) have explained politics as actions or behaviors intended to promote individuals' self-interest that are not explicitly authorized by the organization.

An interesting concept of "political skill" in organizational politics literature has emerged as a new stream to explore, in the recent endeavors by researchers (Andrew, Kacmar and Harris 2009). Political skill refers to "the ability to effectively understand others at work, and to use such knowledge to influence others to act in ways that enhance one's personal and/or organizational objectives" (Ahearn et al. 2004, p. 311). PS of employees plays an imperative role in not only gaining social acceptability and survival, but also in helping to achieve outstanding success in the organization. But some recent research has also proved some adverse behavioral outcomes, such as intent to deceive, in politically skilled employees (Clements, Boyle and Proudfoot 2016). However, PS as a construct has been slightly ignored in terms of situational factors (Andrew et al., 2009), although individual factors have been researched extensively (Liu et al. 2007). But contextual and situational factors have long been suggested as important sources of effectively producing political influence (Ferris and Judge 1991; Valle and Perrewé 2000), and certain situational factors including supervisor behavior could potentially be influenced by the political skill of individuals.

In order to adapt to a given situation, people try to adjust their behavioral responses (Andrew et al. 2009). Therefore, Ferris et al. (2002) indicated the importance of the situational factors to be researched in the paradigm of PS. In this context, environment plays a vital role as a stimulus that modifies and changes the behaviors of the individuals in a given situation (Mischel 1968). In the current study, it is argued that abusive supervision is a situational factor, pertaining within an organization that highlights the importance of good political skill to tackle the situation. Political skill is investigated to work as a resource to hold the abusive behavior of the supervisors. Moreover, as previously studied (Zhang and Bednall 2016), demographic variables are considered to potentially moderate the effect of abusive supervision. Earlier research on workplace aggression also explicitly characterizes the importance of the demographic factors to be studied in this specific area (Aquino and Thau 2009). Zhang and Bednall (2016), suggested that demographic variables have a substantial impact on abusive supervision and its antecedents. Furthermore, Johannsdottir and Olafsson (2004) proposed that established theories provide a rationale for the inclusion of these factors as moderators. Numerous studies have investigated the role of these characteristics, such as gender (Smith, Shu and Madsen 2001), supervisors' experience (Nickerson 1998) and organizational tenure (Conway and Coyle-Shapiro 2012).

The researches investigating the role of subordinates' gender between AS and its antecedents and consequences are scarce and need much attention (Ouyang, Lam and Wang 2015; Cahyono, Haryono, Haryanto, and Harsono 2020). However, as Ng, Chen and Aryee (2012) discussed in their review paper on AS, individual and contextual factors have been thoroughly studied with regard to this specific phenomenon. Yet the demographic variables have not been adequately focused in relation to their effect on abusive supervision. These variables, especially gender, are mostly treated as control variables (Ouyang et al. 2015). As explained in the social role theory (Eagly 1987; 1997), gender may pose a moderating effect on abusive supervision and its relation to other variables (Ouyang et al. 2015). Furthermore, Chukwuorji et al. (2020) has discussed the need for treating gender as a moderator in various social cognition aspects; therefore, subordinate gender is treated as a moderator in the relationship of political skill and abusive supervision. As suggested by Kimura (2015), the intentions of use and effect of political skill might be different for men and women.

The current study augments the research in AS and PS by contributing in a number of ways. First, numerous studies on abusive supervision address the factors instigating the behavior or the negative outcomes as a result of such supervision (Harris et al. 2013; Martinko et al. 2013). In line with this, Zhou, Yang and Spector (2015) contributed by exploring the relationship of PS and workplace aggression. The current study, however, explores the factor of PS through which individuals can potentially avoid or reduce the effect of abusive supervision specifically. It will be empirically shown that certain personality characteristics help in potentially avoiding the negative behavior of supervisors. Secondly, the study will enable supporting the stance that political skill not only results in positive outcomes (Blickle et al. 2011; Laird, Zboja and Ferris 2012) but also reduces the impact of negative outcomes in general. Lastly, this research investigates subordinate gender differences in dealing with abusive supervision, using subordinate political skill. Both males and females possessing good political skill act differently, which ultimately changes the external factors differently for both. This study will highlight how politically skilled men and women face different behavioral responses in same scenarios in organizations.

1.4 Organization of the Dissertation

The structure of the study was planned as follows:

Chapter 1: This chapter discusses the general variables and specific explanations on gaps in literature and significance of the research.

Chapter 2: This chapter gives an in-depth literature review of the study. It includes the hypothesis development and the proposed model.

Chapter 3: Detailed methodology of the parts is explained in this chapter. It includes data description, measures, results, discussion and limitations of the study.

Chapter 4: This chapter discusses the conclusion and policy implications of the research conducted. It also provides future directions for potential studies.

Summary

The chapter covered the introduction of the study by giving the general overview of the role of politics and political skill in organizations. Next the important aspect of the gaps in the literature with reference to this particular study were explained. The problem statement explaining the core issue to be addressed by the study was discussed. Following the problem statement, the significance of the study outcomes was presented. Subsequently, the impacts of political skill on employee level outcomes and supervisor level outcomes were discussed separately. Finally, the organization of the entire thesis with chapter-specific themes was elaborated.

Chapter 2

Literature Review

Introduction

This chapter begins with an introduction to organizational politics. It then reviews the literature on the variables of the study including political skill, perceived organizational politics, abusive supervision, job satisfaction and turnover intention. The next section of the chapter explains the development of the hypothesis on dual levels, employee level outcomes i.e. job satisfaction and turnover intention and supervisor level outcome i.e. abusive supervision. Finally, the theoretical models are discussed.

2.1 Review of the Variables of Study

As defined by Pfeffer (1981), "organizational politics refers to actions taken within the organization in order to acquire, develop, and use power and other resources in a way that will lead to preferred personal outcomes" (Meisler and Vigoda-Gadot 2014). Mintzberg (1985) referred to organizational politics as "the unofficial, narrow-minded, and illegal behaviors of members who attempt to maximize their own benefits by sacrificing benefits to the organizational goal or others" (Park, Kim and Lee 2020). However, most research on the phenomenon has considered its adverse perspective taking into account the lawful actions, misinterpretation and forceful impact (Ferris and King 1991; Mintzberg 1983, 1985). Though the presence of politics in organizations cannot be ignored. Organizations are social units in which individuals and groups struggle to gain benefits in various manners (Molm 1997). Politics in organizations strongly influence the organization's decision-making process (Frank and Feorstl 2018) and budgetary participation (Lau, Scully and Lee 2018). However, Ferris et al. (1989) characterized organizational politics as a behavior intentionally aimed to maximize self-interests. The prominence of self-interest may oppose the general interests of the organization (Vigoda 2000). Therefore, organizational members commonly perceive organizational politics negatively (Vigoda

2000), considering them self-serving and manipulative activities for personal gain at the cost of others (Gandz and Murray 1980; Medison et al. 1980; Drory 1993; Ferris and Kacmar 1992). However, the presence of politics in organizations forces the employees to learn influence tactics for survival and growth. The outcomes of influence tactics are also studied in the literature (Falbe and Yukl 1992). However, more recent research focuses on the impact of political skill (Blickle et al. 2011) and perception of organizational politics (Meisler and Vigoda-Gadot 2014).

2.1.1 Political Skill (PS)

Early research on political aspects labeled organizations as political fields characterized by nepotism and various informal exchanges of favors (Mintberg 1983; Pfeffer 1981). Early researchers (Mintzberg 1983; Pfeffer 1981) emphasized the importance of political skill possessed by the employees in order to maintain successful careers in organizations (Ferris et al. 2008). In this earlier work on organizational politics, focus was largely directed towards the political environment of the organization. However, (Mintzberg (1983) and Pfeffer (1981) were more concerned about the successful survival of an employee in such a scenario. They discussed exploiting the political environment in a favorable way through the use of political savvy.

To conceptualize the nature of political skill (PS), it can be defined as "the ability to effectively understand others at work, and to use such knowledge to influence others to act in ways that enhance one's personal and/or organizational objectives" (Ferris et al. 2005: 127). Later a more theoretical statement on PS characterized it as "a comprehensive pattern of social competencies, with cognitive, affective, and behavioral manifestations, which have both direct effects on outcomes, as well as moderating effects on predictor – outcome relationships" (Ferris et al. 2007: pg. 291). Considering the dire need of development on the PS of employees, Ferris et al. (2005) established a dedicated program to conduct an in-depth investigation on the same.

Individuals possessing PS use their inherent social intelligence to apply to diverse situations in order to appear sincere and trustworthy to influence others (Ferris et al. 2007). Building on the same application, political skill (PS) as a construct was sub-divided in four sub-dimensions including social astuteness, interpersonal influence, networking ability and apparent sincerity (Ferris et al. 2007). Social astuteness states that individuals with high PS are well aware of their social surroundings and the complexities therein. In addition, they are familiar with their own and others' intentions within that scenario (Ferris et al. 2007). Therefore, such individuals have better self-awareness and can accurately infer others' behaviors (Ferris et al. 2012). Since social astuteness exhibits the ability of being sensitive towards others, it inevitably will influence others (Pfeffer 1992). Interpersonal influence means that people who are politically skilled have the ability to easily influence others around them (Ferris et al. 2007). They use their effective and convincing communication skill to make others around them comfortable. Hence, they easily adapt to the situations to get the required outcomes from others (Ferris et al. 2012). Pfeffer (1992) termed this trait as "flexibility" and considered it to be very important. Individuals with high PS are proficient in building diverse relationships and can even manipulate associations and friendships as strong bonds, a skill known as networking ability (Ferris et al. 2012). This ability allows them build huge networks to support them as they strive to attain their objectives. In addition, individuals proficient in

PS know how to make their network powerful by networking with influential people to produce opportunities (Pfeffer 1992). Ferris et al. (2012) also acknowledged the ability of conflict handling and negotiations of politically skilled people to ensure strong bonds with others. Due to their apparent sincerity, people perceive these politically skilled individuals as being of high integrity and genuine in their conduct (Ferris et al. 2012). Because of this impression, their effort to influence others is treated as positive and reliable (Ferris et al. 2007). This impression, however, hides any personal motive of the influencer since the level of trust of others is so high. Jones (1990) proposed apparent sincerity as one of the reasons for the successful influence of politically skilled individuals.

While discussing the historical development of PS construct, it can be safely said that Pfeffer (1981) was the first scholar to introduce the term "political skill". His concept of power was objective in nature and he considered power as a resource to be acquired, used and developed through PS. He further pointed out the need for extensive work to be carried out on this construct (Pfeffer 1981). Interestingly, Mintzberg (1983, 1985) was carrying out a similar but independent research in the same field. He proposed that political players (referred to as "influencers") have the will and skill to acquire power. He explained the new construct in this way: "Political skill means the ability to use the bases of power effectively - to convince those to whom one has access, to use one's resources, information, and technical skills to their fullest in bargaining, to exercise formal power with a sensitivity to the feelings of others, to know where to concentrate one's energies, to sense what is possible, to organize the necessary alliances". This clearly relates power and political skill with formal power in the organization (Perrewé et al. 2004). Subsequent to the initial work on PS in 1980s, little attention was devoted to the construct until the end of the 1990s. After this long gap, Ferris et al. (1999) highlighted that not only was the "what" of influence, comprising political tactics and behavior, important, but so was the "how" of influence, i.e. the skill component, and that together they had considerable importance in politics literature. This particular research was much influenced by Jones (1990), who suggested that knowledge about tactics, strategies and form of influence might be adequate, but how to deliver and execute the influence attempt was much under-investigated though very crucial (Ferris et al. 2012). The milestone achieved during the 1990s by Ferris et al. (1999) was undoubtedly the development of the first six item scale of "Political Skill Inventory (PSI)" to measure the construct. However, it was an initial structure and later underwent numerous refinements. The next decade was marked by an exponential increase in the research on political skill. After the development of an initial scale by Ferris et al. (1999), struggles were directed towards the development of a more comprehensive and multi-dimensional measure of PS. These efforts ultimately resulted in the development of a four dimensional and 18-item construct of political skill by Ferris et al. (2005).

While later tremendous growth on PS research was marked as discussed in the next paragraphs, negligible efforts were exerted towards the potential antecedents (Ferris et al. 2008). On the call of Kolodinsky, Hochwarter and Ferris (2004), research was conducted in which extraversion and proactive personality were identified as personality predictors of PS (Liu et al. 2007). Empirical findings indicated that proactive personality would serve as an antecedent of PS (Shi, Chen and Zhou 2011). Though Ferris et al. (2008) called for additional investigation of the predictors of PS, their work on the identification and development of PS antecedents started earlier. They suggested perceptiveness, control, affability and active influence as four themes to present as primary conceptualizations for predicting PS (Ferris et al. 2008). However, they explained that personality traits are not the only factors influencing PS; rather, it can be established as a learned behavior through experience (Ferris et al. 2008).

Political skill has been associated with favorable outcomes for those possessing and utilizing it properly. Employees with good PS are generally able to have positive relations with peers, subordinates and supervisors. Bing et al. (2011) in a quantitative review, concluded a positive relationship of PS with task and conceptual performance. Also in literature various researches proved a significantly positive relationship between PS and job satisfaction (Banister and Meriac 2015; Taliadorou and Pashiadris 2015) whereas negative relation between PS and turnover intention (Banister and Meriac 2015). On similar lines, Munyon et al. (2015) in their meta-analysis controlled the Big Five personality characteristics on the PS and performance relationship. They presented insightful directions for future research in the same area of political skill in their analysis (Munyon et al. 2015). Munyon et al. (2015) have explained PS as a function of three processes, including interpersonal process, behavioral process and intra-psychic process. However, political skill has been positively associated with impression management in literature using interpersonal process (Treadway et al. 2007). In a recent study, the other two processes, intra-psychic and behavioral, have also been investigated to strengthen impression management tactics in people with high PS (Maher et al. 2018). Several studies also tested the mediating role of job satisfaction for the relationship of PS and various outcomes (Wang and McChamp 2019; Li, Sun and Cheng 2017). García-Chas, Neira-Fontela, Varela-Neira, and Curto- Rodríguez (2019) also tested the effect of employee political skill on the intention to leave with the mediation of perceived organizational support.

The application of political skill is not limited to professional life; however, negligible research on the impact of PS on social life has been conducted (Wang and Hall 2019). Therefore, the social impact of PS was investigated in a recent study by Wang and Hall (2019). In order to exclude the workplace factor, data were collected from the participants in laboratory settings, eliminating all the work-related references and including personality questionnaires (Wang and Hall 2019). The results indicated positive personal ratings of social life quality, likeability from perceivers' perspective and positive sociality rated by friends (Wang and Hall 2019). However, while the results on personal ratings of social quality life became insignificant when social self-efficacy, extraversion and self-monitoring were controlled, the other two findings remained significant (Wang and Hall 2019).

Employees in organizations vary from one another with respect to their personalities and backgrounds. Toxic employees are those who have high "dark triad" i.e. high in Machiavellianism, narcissism, and/or psychopathy (Paulhus and Williams 2002; Jonason, Slomski and Partyka 2012). In a recent study, toxic people high in PS were associated with higher performance rating by supervisors, resulting in high salaries and promotion opportunities (Templer 2018) as they are better able to modify their behaviors to be socially and contextually suitable (Baloch et al. 2017). Though it was argued that regardless of the actual performance of dark triad employees, they are rated higher by using their political skill through casting a positive self-rating due to their inherent shrewdness (Templer 2018). In another study, Baloch et al. (2017) investigated that dark triad individuals usually have high PS and therefore, they perceive more politics in the organization. Due to their keen perception of politics, they easily gain political advantages using their networking ability and social astuteness, as they have strong PS (Baloch et al. 2017).

Recently Kimura, Bande and Fernández-Ferrín (2019) identified the lack of research attention on the skills of salespeople as a predictor of effective adaptive selling. Numerous researchers have investigated the role of externally-directed and intra-organizational behavior on adaptive selling of salespeople (Plouffe and Barclay 2007). However, drawing on social exchange theory, social capital theory and social cognitive theory, all the four dimensions of PS allow salespeople to effectively adaptive selling behavior (Kimura et al. 2019). High PS salespeople cognitively analyze influence tactics, reactions and impressions on the customers to respond accordingly without giving the impression of treachery or deceit (Kimura et al. 2019).

Summers et al. (2020), in the recent meta-analysis on the effects of PS on stressor and strain processes, tried to sort out the contradictory and inconsistent results by estimating the meta-analytic effect sizes of PS. They concluded that there was a negative relationship between PS and stressors, and ultimately also with strain responses (Summers et al. 2020). Preceding in the study, utilization of personal resources as a buffer to minimize the impact of stressors on workplace outcomes was investigated, where PS was used as a personal resource (Karatepe, Kim and Lee 2019). Personal resources help to mitigate the adverse effects of stressors on strain (Hobfoll 2001). Drawing on the same rationale, PS was investigated as a way of decreasing the negative impact of supervisor and coworker incivility, leading to emotional exhaustion (EE), and on organizational citizenship behavior (OCB) (Karatepe et al. 2019). The subjective evaluation of impolite behavior of bosses and peers aggravates EE, and therefore, employees facing such situations try to avoid the strain by utilizing their personal valued resources (Karatepe et al. 2019). To support the relationship, Harvey et al. (2007) have indicated the application of conservation of resources theory to explain the moderating role of PS.

In another study, PS has been investigated as a way of mitigating the adverse effect of workplace ostracism (social exclusion) by reducing counter-productive work behaviors with the interplay of a proactive personality (Zhao, Peng and Sheard 2013). The negative outcomes of workplace ostracism for high politically skilled individuals are low for a high proactive personality as compared to a low proactive personality (Zhao et al. 2013). Since politically skilled people are socially astute with high interpersonal influence, they effortlessly respond to any situation including ostracized conditions (Ferris et al. 2007). However, for individuals with low political skill, the relationship between ostracism and negative outcomes will be stronger (Zhao et al. 2013) as they may not be able to respond to the strain and stress caused by workplace ostracism (Leung et al. 2011). Earlier, in another study, PS was observed to neutralize the effects of perceived role conflict on strain, such that high PS (as a moderator) reduced the undesirable effects of role conflict (Perrewe et al. 2004).

Individuals strong in PS not only have the talent to decrease the uncertainty prevailing in political conditions, but they are also able to minimize the associated negative consequences or maximize positive returns (Kacmar et al. 2013). Since organizational politics provide a conducive environment to operationalize PS, high politically skilled people have a positive view of perceived organizational politics (POP) (Mintzberg 1983). Moreover, the inherent astuteness of PS individuals high in PS weakens the POP and negative outcomes relationship (Kacmar et al. 2013). On the other hand, individuals with low PS are unable to view POP as an opportunity, and therefore they experience more negative outcomes as compared to high politically skilled individuals (Kacmar et al. 2013).

In another study, PS as a moderator in cross-national contexts (United States and Greece) was examined to have potential impact on POP and job performance (Kapoutsis et al. 2011). It was investigated whether or not individuals with strong PS in low politically perceived organization will show superior job performance (Kapoutsis et al. 2011). The rationale presented was that people with high PS will utilize their excess resources in a more effective way, rather than utilizing it to analyze and respond to political situations (Treadway et al. 2005). As per the results of the study, settings with high perception of politics showed no change in job performance with employees possessing high PS, whereas low POP with high PS showed significant increase in job performance among the employees (Kapoutsis et al. 2011). Also, Brouer et al. (2006) demonstrated the buffering effect of PS on the work stressor i.e. organizational politics.

Meurs et al. (2010) in their study investigated that political skill helps to reduce the perceived strain on the affected individuals, basing their argument on the reasoning that high PS provides individuals with better ability to interact with others and to achieve objectives. In another study, the negative impact of social stressors was buffered by PS to result in enhanced job and career satisfaction (Harvey et al. 2007). PS has been linked negatively with cognitive and somatic anxiety (Perrewe et al. 2004). Perrewe et al. (2005) showed that PS moderates the associations among role overload and job tension, satisfaction and anxiety. Also, employees with good PS use it for personal favors but are not perceived as manipulators by their bosses (Treadway et al. 2007).

In a research study, Jawahar et al. (2007) demonstrated the dual effect of PS and perception of organizational support, drawing on conservation of resources theory. They discussed the direct impact of PS on emotional exhaustion, depersonalization and personal accomplishment, and the moderating effect of PS on the relationship of burnout and emotional exhaustion, depersonalization and personal accomplishment (Jawahar et al. 2007). However, PS was linked with decreased personal accomplishment and depersonalization. It also moderated the personal accomplishment relationship (Jawahar et al. 2007)

2.1.2 Perceived Organizational Politics (POP)

Ferris and Kacmar (1992) explained perceived organizational politics as the subjective evaluation by the employees of the politics in a given organization, building on the assertions of the early theorists including Gandz and Murray (1980). Fundamentally, it is the perception of the individuals regarding the politics that influences their behavioral outcomes rather than the actual politics (Ferris and Kacmar 1992). Based on this assumption, Ferris et al. (2000) suggested that perceived organizational politics "involves an individual's attribution to behaviors of self-serving intent, and is defined as an individual's subjective evaluation about the extent to which the work environment is characterized by coworkers and supervisors who demonstrate such self-serving behavior." In the words of Kacmar and Carlson (1997), "POP refers to one's perception of the political activities of members other than oneself within an organization, and it signifies the degree to which each member perceives the work environment as political"

(Park, Kim and Lee 2020). Perceived organizational politics has been explained in three dimensions, namely: going along to get ahead, pay and promotion policies and general political behavior (Kacmar and Carlson 1997).

Initially presented by Ferris et al. (1989), perceived organizational politics (POP) has been a field of keen importance for researchers during the past couple of decades (Meisler and Vigoda-Gadot 2014). In the earlier study, several factors including organizational, environmental and personal dynamics proved to be the stimulators of POP that lead to several organizational outcomes (Ferris et al. 1989). Studies have established that individuals who observe politics at work face adverse outcomes including decreased job satisfaction and organizational commitment (Vigoda 2000), poor performance (Chang et al. 2009), and turnover intentions (Miller et al. 2008). In a recent study, abusive supervision, POP and political behavior were investigated for potential associations (Liu et al. 2018). Abusive supervision produces an ambiguous environment for employees (Thau et al. 2009) which supports the employees' perception of organizational politics (Liu et al. 2018). To successfully operate in a political environment, employees exhibit political behavior as a resource to cope with various uncertainties (Ferris et al. 1989). Therefore, abusive supervision leads to political behavior with POP as a mediator (Liu et al. 2018).

Ferris et al. (1989) presented a model for organizational politics which can serve as a base for various POP related negative outcomes and different antecedents (Vigoda 2000). As in earlier research, positive affectivity (PA) and negative affectivity (NA) were investigated to influence POP (Ferris et al. 2002). Moreover, another study investigated the moderating effect of PA/NA and POP (Hochwarter and Treadway 2003). The outcomes of the study supported the interaction effect of PA/NA between the association of POP and job satisfaction (Hochwarter and Treadway 2003).

Among several studies investigating negative outcomes of POP, Chang et al. (2009) explored several undesirable effects of POP in their meta-analysis. Perceived organizational politics has been linked to increased turnover intentions in employees (Chang et al. 2009). Since employees may not see the political environment as conducive to work, job performance is also hampered (Chang et al. 2009; Park 2016). Moreover, strain is positively influenced causing lower levels of job satisfaction (JS), affective commitment, and organizational citizenship behavior (Chang et al. 2009).

In a recent study, POP has been positively linked to knowledge hiding (Malik et al. 2019). Based on the Job Demands-Resources Model by Bakker and Demerouti (2007), which proposes two characteristics i.e. job demands and job resources to impact employee well-being (Demerouti et al. 2001), the study considers organizational politics as job demands (Malik et al. 2019). Since job demands are the characteristics of any job which require persistent struggle, the job demands lead to withdrawal behaviors and/ or psychological/ physiological costs (Bakker and Demerouti 2007). Drawing on the same rationale, the study suggested that individuals facing perceived organizational politics intentionally hide/ withhold the required information (known as knowledge hiding) from the organization (Malik et al. 2019). Employees hold the information in a difficult political environment for three primary reasons, which are protecting self-interest, acquiring power or as a defensive behavior (Malik et al. 2019). Knowledge hiding further leads to lower employee creativity, which has an adverse impact on an organization in today's innovation-oriented world (Malik et al. 2019).

An insightful argument by Kacmar and Ferris (1991) suggested that individuals with high POP in the organization will have a low perception level of equity, justice and fairness in the organization. Following this, the theory of procedural justice was applied to establish that organizational politics is related to the efficiency of human resource systems and decision-making (Folger et al. 1992). Where the perception of politics was higher, justice and fairness were deficient in human resource and decision-making, resulting in adverse consequences for the organization (Vigoda 2000). As discussed in the earlier section, the perception of the reality, rather the reality per se, affects individual behavior (Lewin 1936). However, perception of justice and fairness is also an indication of the political environment of the organization (Vigoda 2000).

Literature on politics in organizations has paid special attention to POP or personal advancement tactics (Park et al. 2020). Individuals highly involved in political activities create a high perception of politics for those with lower involvement in such political conduct (Park et al. 2020). Unfair political activities potentially increase stress (Ferris et al. 1989) and employees also treat politics as a work-related stressor (Park et al. 2020). Hobfoll (1989) presented the conservation of resources theory, which explained that high job demand or deficient resources at work are balanced by employees through their extra effort. Ultimately, when the job demands (politics in POP) are very high, the existing resources possessed by the employees deplete, resulting in stress and anxiety.

In recent research, the relationship between POP and self-determined work motivation was extensively studied (Cho and Yang 2018). The propositions presented, namely that politics in organizations is a key determinant of self-determined motivation, and work mood mediates the earlier relationship, were based on affective events theory, self-determination theory and emotion-associated theories (Cho and Yang 2018). The results, however, indicated that POP determines work moods which in turn influence behavioral outcomes in organizations (Cho and Yang 2018).

A reasonable focus on the emotional implications of politics in organizations is missing in the literature, even though people participating in and experiencing politics go through deep emotional upheavals (Meisler and Vigoda-Gadot 2014). However, certain studies now take into account this side. Applying affective events theory (Weiss and Cropanzano 1996), which states that employees' attitudes and behaviors are affected by emotional experiences, emotional behaviors were studied to mediate the link between POP and behavioral outcomes (Liu et al. 2006). Personal or peer political behavior serves as an instigator for the arousal of emotional reactions which in turn results in adverse outcomes, including decreased commitment and satisfaction (Liu et al. 2006; Rosen et al. 2009). In a study, POP and job satisfaction were partially mediated by frustration, which further affects performance, citizenship behavior and intention to quit (Rosen et al. 2009). Another study suggests POP as a mediator between emotional intelligence and workplace outcomes (Meisler and Vigoda-Gadot 2014).

2.1.3 Abusive Supervision

Research into the dark side of leadership has focused on a number of issues, with a relatively recent phenomenon highlighted by Tepper (2000) garnering immense attention. Tepper (2000) defined the term abusive supervision (AS) as "subordinates' perceptions of the extent to which supervisors engage in the sustained display of hostile verbal and nonverbal behaviors, excluding physical contact". However, as per the definition, it is the perception of the victim that depicts the subjective nature of the concept (Tepper 2000). Such perception varies from context to context and person to person. Individuals may have a different perception about a supervisor's behavior in different contexts, and two individuals may treat a specific action differently (Tepper 2000). For instance, a person may feel humiliated when he or she has been treated harshly in a group and not when alone. Similarly, a very sensitive individual may take a simple rejection as abusive treatment while another may take it as simply feedback. AS has been clearly identified as a separate and distinct phenomenon from petty tyranny, hostility, and aggression (Tepper 2000). Jezl et al. (1996) and Shepard and Campbell (1992) presented AS as a continuing and permanent phenomenon till the victim dismisses the relationship or the perpetrator ends the relationship or the perpetrator changes his or her behavior (Tepper 2000). However, the sustainability of abusive supervision is due to various factors. From a victim's point of view, they bear with such behavior because they are powerless, economically dependent, frightened of the consequences and hopeful that the behavior will end someday (Walker 1979). From a perpetrator's point of view, the perpetrators are unable to identify, modify and alter their behavior (Wolfe 1987).

Abusive supervision has been linked with a number of undesirable consequences for subordinates comprising chronic stress (Tepper 2007), psychological distress and low organizational commitment (Duffy, Ganster and Pagon 2002), low job satisfaction (Tepper 2000), turnover intention (Lyu et al. 2019), work and job withdrawal (Atwater et al. 2016), supervisor directed deviance (Restubog et al. 2011), low contextual performance (Aryee et al. 2008), family satisfaction, work-to-family conflict and relationship tension (Carlson et al. 2011) and low creativity (Han, Harms and Bai 2017).

Abusive supervision has recently been investigated to have psychiatric impact, such as paranoia, on victims as well (Bortolon et al. 2019). In an earlier study, paranoia has been associated with perceived social support, stress and low levels of social cohesion (Freeman et al. 2011). However, in the prevalence of abusive context, the results may get even worse (Bortolon et al. 2019). Also AS has numerous adverse emotional and behavioral consequences (Aryee et al. 2008; Carlson et al. 2012). Chan and McAllister (2014) proposed the relationship of abuse and paranoia since employees try to cope with abuse by triggering paranoid thoughts of scanning the environment to detect threat-related information.

In another study, AS was proposed to moderate the association between resilience and turnover intention and work engagement (Dai, Zhuang and Huan 2019). Drawing on the self-determination theory (Deci and Ryan 2002), it was proposed that abusive supervision as a situational factor impacts the relation between resilience and intention to leave and work engagement (Dai et al. 2019). The results of the research suggested that a resilient employee will show lesser intention to leave and higher work engagement in low abusive supervision as compared to high (Dai et al. 2019). Though abusive supervision has various adverse outcomes on subordinates, managers themselves achieve a high sense of power and self-efficacy (Ju et al. 2019).

In a recent study, AS was proposed to predict service sabotage by the employees in hospitality industry (Park and Kim 2019). Service sabotage, which refers to intentional harm to customer service in the service provision industry (Harris and Ogbonna 2006), negatively affects organizational performance. Applying the theory of displaced aggression (Dollard et al. 1939), it was proposed that when subordinates are not able to react against the perpetrator of abuse, they vent their frustration on the easiest and most convenient target available to them (Park and Kim 2019). Moreover, the victim considers the treatment of abuse from the organization rather than from a particular person, thus taking abuse as psychological contract breach, which mediates abusive supervision and service sabotage (Park and Kim 2019). In general, abusive supervision is related to negative outcomes. However, in a recent study, AS was associated with an intent to achieve pro-organizational goals (Watkins et al. 2019).

Abusive supervision has various adverse outcomes, without any doubt. However, to control the negative consequences, the antecedents of abusive supervision need to be addressed first (Tepper et al. 2017). From a managerial perspective, if organizations need to overcome this issue, the research on the predictors of AS will be helpful to enable them to avoid such instances (Tepper et al. 2017). Regarding the importance of the causes of AS, a tremendous growth in the literature from this perspective has occurred in the last decade. This research can be divided into three areas, namely social learning, identity threat and self-regulation impairment (Tepper et al. 2017). Drawing on the social learning theory (Bandura 1973), it is argued that individuals acquire various behaviors and attitudes through environmental observation and consider them acceptable norms to follow (Tepper et al. 2017). People are inspired by those who have high rank and integrity and use them as role models. Moreover, relevant organizational features (like culture) also affect the learning orientation (Tepper et al. 2017). The upper management in a given organization are considered influential by the subordinates (Brown et al. 2005). Following this rationale, studies show a trickle-down approach of AS (Mawritz et al. 2012). Liu et al. (2012) argued that middle-level managers' emulation is dependent on the intention of upper-level managers for abusive behavior such that abuse for better performance trickles down more. However, the workplace is not the first social unit an individual enters; in fact, basic upbringing starts at home (Tepper et al. 2017). Therefore, the first role model for some people may be their parents (Bandura 1973). Aggressive behavior learnt at home may assert itself at work at later stages as an acceptable custom, and research has also shown a significant association between AS and family undermining experience (Kiewitz et al. 2012). Furthermore, contextual factors also influence behavioral modifications in individuals. Organizational norms play an important role in explaining the abusive supervisory behavior (Tepper et al. 2017). Aggressive norms in organizations positively predict abusive supervision (Restubog et al. 2011; Zhang and Bednall 2016). The culture of the country also predicts abusive supervisory behavior (Tepper et al. 2017). Vogel et al. (2015) discussed the difference in acceptability level of hostile behavior in different cultures. The literature also sheds light on the fact that people of Asian countries as compared to people in the United States generally face more abusive supervision (Mackey et al. 2017).

Supervisors can demonstrate abusive behavior when their identity as a leader or their authority and competency is challenged by their subordinates (Tepper et al. 2017). According to the social interactionist theory of aggression (Tedeschi and Felson 1994), people consider hostile behavior as a coping strategy, when they are unable to fulfill their desired identity in a given situation. Hostile behavior can take the form of AS (Tepper et al. 2017). With any elevation in the career growth of professionals, the pressure to sustain the competency increases; however, it may be threatened by subordinates, higher authorities or from their own feelings of experiencing identity risk (Tepper et al. 2017).

The performance of the supervisor is somehow dependent on the performance and output of the direct subordinates. Therefore, poor performance of the subordinates may result in perception of identity threat for the supervisor (Tepper et al. 2017). Tepper et al. (2017) presented two theoretical lenses for determining abusive behavior of supervisors towards low performing subordinates which are, victim precipitation theory and moral exclusion theory. Based on the same theoretical lenses, various researchers have found a significant relation between AS and low employee performance (Liang et al. 2016; Wang et al. 2016). However, Khan et al. (2016) have presented an interesting insight by establishing a model where the high performers suffer from AS, and where supervisors have a high social dominance orientation as a personality trait, which in turn causes the supervisors to perceive the reports as potential threats to the existing hierarchy of the organization. Therefore, along with the performance of the subordinate, the personality of the supervisor plays an important role in determining the behavioral actions of the supervisor. Tepper et al. (2006) discussed that when supervisors face threats and stress from the top hierarchy in the organizations, they respond to such behaviors by treating their subordinates abusively as safe targets for them. This phenomenon of expressing frustration against less powerful targets has been referred to as displaced aggression (Tedeschi and Norman 1985). However, displaced aggression emerges in critical circumstances which then causes AS (Tepper et al. 2017). The third source of threat for identity may arise from within the supervisor i.e. supervisor characteristics. Johnson et al. (2012) have linked strong individual identity with abusive supervision. Moreover, psychological entitlement of the supervisor has also been linked to abusive outbursts (Whitman, Halbesleben and Shanine 2013). In addition, Machiavellianism directly predicts abusive supervision, with authoritarian leadership style as a mediator as well (Kiazad et al. 2010). However, in a recent study by Greenbaum et al. (2017), AS has been proposed as a predictor of Machiavellianism which results in unethical behavior.

The last reason highlighted by Tepper et al. (2017) for AS is related to self-regulation impairment. To explain self-regulation impairment, an understanding of self-regulation is important. Self-regulation is defined as the consistency between behavior and associated outcomes (Swann 2012). With a functional self-regulation process, individuals can identify outcomes and the impact of their behavior, modifying any deviation in their behavior when the results become undesirable (Carver 1979; Carver and Scheier 1982). However, in any attempt to self-regulate, personal resources are consumed which are already scarce due the demand of resources at work (Tepper et al. 2017). Particularly, in a supervisory position the demand and consumption of these resources increases tremendously (Yam et al. 2016). Therefore, depletion of resources causes personal incapability to self-regulate (Tepper et al. 2017), which in turn leads to regulatory failure involving negative behavioral outbursts (Baumeister et al. 2007). Ego depletion theory has also been used by various scholars to explain abusive supervision (Tepper et al. 2017). For instance, Barnes et al. (2015) proposed that the quantity and quality of sleep affects leaders' abusive outbursts due to ego depletion.

2.1.4 Job Satisfaction

Job satisfaction (JS) is a notion grounded on the person's evaluation of the job that he or she is doing (Ilies and Judge 2004). Therefore, it depends upon a number of factors including experience, promotion, and salary (Zhao, Hwang and Lim 2020). Dunnette and Locke (1976) have defined JS as a "pleasurable emotional state resulting from appraisal of one's job or job experience". Also "job satisfaction is the pleasurable emotional state resulting from the achievement of one's job values in the work situation" (Locke and Henne 1986). Mahdi et al. (2012) stated that when an employee feels his job is fulfilling or enables him or her to fulfill important job values that are compatible with needs, a positive emotion emerges resulting in higher job satisfaction levels (Dunnette and Locke 1976). Basically, job satisfaction reflects how rewarding the job of a person is in terms of the value of the reward to him or her (Mahdi et al. 2012), and it is connected to the general attitude of the person towards the job (Robbins 2003). It can be treated as a person's affective response to work condition aspects and work roles held (Williams and Hazer 1986; Mottaz 1988; Glick 1992).

One of the most important theories explaining causes of job satisfaction is the two-factor (motivation and hygiene) theory presented by Herzberg, Mausner and Snyderman (1959). The concept explains two core components of work satisfaction i.e. intrinsic factors and extrinsic factors. Intrinsic factors, also known as motivators, denotes content, which includes achievement, promotion, work content, responsibility, and recognition. Extrinsic factors, also called hygiene, are context related, and include the policy and administration of a company, technical supervision, working conditions, payment and interpersonal supervision. Additionally, the theory explained the difference between JS and job dissatisfaction. Herberg et al. (1959) claimed that the opposite of job satisfaction is not dissatisfaction but is rather no satisfaction, as it is not necessary that an employee who is not satisfied has to be dissatisfied. Further, they proposed that the motivators ensure JS, whereas hygiene factors ensure no dissatisfaction. To further extend the work on this two-factor theory, Hackman and Oldham (1980) presented the role of personal characteristics of the employees for explaining JS levels. They claimed that it is not only the motivators (intrinsic factors) and hygiene (extrinsic factors) that impact job satisfaction levels of the employees; in fact, knowledge, skills, and need for growth are some of the personal factors that influence satisfaction levels.

Ling and Loo (2015) in their study, drawn on job characteristics theory, identified salary, autonomy and task value as important job characteristics, and knowledge, skills, job fit, elevation opportunities and self-development as personal characteristics that affect JS. Other influencing factors of JS including motivation (Ferris et al. 2013) and safety priority along with organizational effectiveness, fair rewards, resource adequacy, job tenure, and physical and mental health (Shan et al. 2016).

Recently while focusing on job characteristics regarding JS, Wang et al. (2020) studied the association between workplace IT and IT satisfaction of the employee with JS. The study is interesting with respect to the attempt it made to combine job-related characteristics and behavioral outcomes. The research based the relation on satisfaction spillover theory, where employee satisfaction with workplace IT systems predicts job satisfaction (Wang et al. 2020). The study findings revealed a significant relation between IT satisfaction and JS. Moreover, job fit as mediator and professional fit as moderator showed significant impact as well (Wang et al. 2020).

In another research study, boss phubbing (use of cell phone while communicating with a subordinate) has been investigated to affect performance of the employee through job satisfaction and supervisory trust (Roberts and David 2020). Applying the reciprocated social exchange theory, expectancy violations theory and social presence theory, the study proved a sequential mediation, where boss phubbing negatively influences job performance through low supervisory trust and JS (Roberts and David 2020). Liu et al. (2019) investigated a positive impact of personal competencies, job adaptation and social adaptation on JS. Moreover, anger control significantly determines JS, such that high anger control results in high JS levels (La and Yun 2019). Furthermore, task identity and autonomy (from the job characteristics model) positively predicts thriving at work, which further displays a positive relation with job satisfaction (Jiang et al. 2020). Inegbedion et al. (2020) explained the relationship of workload balance and JS. Numerous studies have shown a clear relationship of job satisfaction and work performance (Ling and Loo 2015; Ton and Huckman 2008). Also, high productivity and low stress levels and turnover have been linked with job satisfaction (Shan et al. 2016). In a recent study, job satisfaction positively predicted the enthusiasm levels of the employees (Buric and Moe 2020). Akimak and Ayla (2019) explained the effect of balanced time perspective on burnout to further influence JS levels.

2.1.5 Turnover Intention

Turnover intention (TI) has been referred to as a conscious and well considered willfulness to quit the organization (Tett and Meyer 1993). TI is considered to be a very strong phase where employee usually end up actually leaving the organization. It is considered the last step of the withdrawal process following thinking to quit the job and looking for job alternatives (Mobley, Homer and Hollingsworth 1978). However, actual turnover results in the termination of the employee's job with the organization (Tett and Meyer 1993). TI has been recognized as a significantly major predictor of turnover, and various research has confirmed the association between the two (Joo and Park 2010). In earlier studies on the link amid turnover and turnover intention, scholars have highlighted behavioral intentions as sole dependable antecedent of actual turnover or leaving (Bluedorn 1982; Lee and Mowday 1987). Since, the intention to leave is a voluntary decision where the employee is not forced to leave the job, it is very important to understand the various factors that may impact or instigate such intentions in employees.

Moreover, turnover has a deleterious impact on organizations. In a study, Addae et al. (2006) claimed that turnover intention leads to actual turnover which costs the organization in two ways i.e. cost of hiring a new employee and cost of disruption in workflow. Since hiring and training an employee is expensive to the organization, the financial cost borne by the organization affects the performance of the organization. Furthermore, when a trained employee leaves the job, it takes a little while to fill the position of that employee with another equally competent person. The lag in finding the right person for the job also decreases the performance levels of the organization.

Since turnover intention and actual turnover has proved to be a detrimental phenomenon for organizational growth and performance, the factors affecting the employees' intentions to quit the job have been thoroughly addressed in the literature. One of the most studied relations in turnover literature is between job satisfaction and turnover intention. Career and job satisfaction have been identified as a major predictor of turnover in employees (Egan, Yang and Bartlett 2004; Wright and Bonnet 2007). Wright and Bonnet (2007) indicated a high probability of employee turnover in the presence of low psychological well-being and job satisfaction. In contrast, in a different study, level of satisfaction with promotion opportunities and work meaningfulness significantly predicted less turnover intention (Wright and Bonnet 1992).

Organizational commitment is an important employee related behavior, and therefore, numerous studies have investigated the outcomes of organizational commitment (Joo and Park 2010). Meyer and Allen (1997) in their study investigated the relationship of organizational commitment to turnover. They found that individuals with a high level of commitment towards the organization will have a low intention to quit the organization even in difficult circumstances. In another study, intrinsic motivation was investigated to decrease turnover intention (Richer, Blanchard and Vallerand 2002). The study indicated that intrinsic motivation decreases emotional exhaustion, which in turn increases satisfaction levels (Richer et al. 2002). As discussed earlier, job satisfaction predicts turnover intention, as was confirmed in the study conducted by Richer et al. (2002). Specifically, in the public sector, when employees are offered high intrinsic motivation and job involvement, their intention to quit the job decreases (Bertelli 2007). Moynihan and Landuyt (2008) discussed the negative relationship of diversity policies and turnover intention of public sector employees. Also, in another study, turnover was proved to be reduced with better advancement opportunities in government sector employees (Kim 2005).

This section shed light on the literature of the study variables by explaining their nature, causes and consequences. In the next part, relationships and hypotheses of the discussed variables will be linked up based on the theories and arguments discussed and proved in the literature. First, the impact of PS on employee level outcomes including job satisfaction and turnover intention is developed, grounded in the theoretical lenses. Moreover, perceived organizational politics is treated as the moderator on the developed relation. Second, the impact of political skill on supervisor level outcomes is discussed, specifically in relation to abusive supervision.

2.2 Political Skill, Organizational Politics and its Outcomes

2.2.1 Political Skill and Job Satisfaction

Politics in organizations is a highly debatable concept (Vigoda and Cohen 2002). Political skill (PS) is viewed as a set of positive traits needed for effective relationships and/or influence within the organization. Literature has strongly supported the notion that to professionally excel in political workplace conditions, PS is a much-needed trait (Pfeffer 1981). Previous research significantly supports the positive outcomes of PS (Treadway et al. 2004; Brouer et al. 2006; Ferris et al. 2007).

In order to get a better understanding, Ferris et al. (2007) explained four dimensions that constitute PS traits in an individual. These are social astuteness, interpersonal influence, apparent sincerity, and networking (Ferris et al. 2007). Individuals proficient in PS use their inherent astuteness and networking ability to understand the environment of the workplace and motives of others around them (Brouer, Harris and Kacmar 2011). As they develop strong networks, they are able to dig out important information from others (Treadway et al. 2004). Since they have all the important information available, they are able to identify what is expected from them to ensure their own success (Brouer et al. 2011). Consequently, individuals having good PS find the organizational setup as a productive avenue to exploit their own skills to accomplish personal goals (Ferris et al. 2007). These individuals, therefore, evaluate their work environment positively which is reflected in their higher levels of JS (Locke 1970). Job Satisfaction (JS) is "one's affective attachment to the job viewed either in its entirety (global satisfaction) or with regard to particular aspects (facet satisfaction; e.g., supervision)" (Tett and Meyer 1993: 261). However, JS itself is a multifaceted function consisting of diverse factors including financial benefits, participation in decision making and leadership style (March and Simon 1958). In three different studies, Kolodindsky, Hochwarter and Ferris (2004) verified a positive relationship between PS and JS. Thus, with respect to employees' personal attributes and skills, JS is interesting to explore. It is therefore feasible to study individuals' PS as an antecedent of employee JS. Meisler (2014) and a meta-analysis by Munyon et al. (2015) reported a positive relationship between PS and JS. Hence, we hypothesize;

> *H1:*   *There is a positive relationship between the political skill of employees and their job satisfaction.*

2.2.2 Job Satisfaction and Turnover Intention

Job satisfaction is referred to as "a pleasurable or positive emotional state resulting from the appraisal of one's job" (Dunnette and Locke 1976, p. 1300). The positive feeling emerges when a person perceives his job as fulfilling or allowing him to accomplish his job values (Dunnette and Locke 1976). However, the values must be desirable and compelling for that individual (Locke 1969), since the values not desired or needed by the employees may not provide pleasure or gratification. Studies of organizational attitudes consider JS as a very important work attitude (Weiss 2002). A number of positive work outcomes have been investigated in the literature associated with JS. As an emotional state, its importance in an employee's life cannot be underestimated (Alegre, Mas-Machuca and Berbegal-Mirabent 2016). With positive sets of emotions, employees can be more loyal and committed to the organization. Moreover, a company's performance is directly influenced by motivated employees (Kowal and Roztocki 2015). JS has been categorized as a complex phenomenon composed of various factors i.e., it is influenced by monetary, participatory, and leading dynamics (March and Simon 1958). Also, Herzberg's two factor theory has explained a number of intrinsic and extrinsic factors influencing JS levels. In the same research, March and Simon (1958) proposed the idea that JS will lessen the desire of employees to quit the job, consequently reducing turnover. In contrast, further literature has indicated that when employees' expectations are not met, employees tend to leave due to dissatisfaction.

Early development of TI research had already identified desire to leave (JS) and ease of leaving (alternative jobs available) as two main reasons for turnover intention (March and Simon 1958). Since desire to leave is an emotional state, many researchers relate it to job satisfaction. JS is clearly a significant psychological predictor of TI (Dickter, Roznowski and Harrison 1996). Lee et al. (1999), in their study, considered JS as a major predictor in almost all the turnover theories. Recent studies have shown a significantly negative association between JS and TI (Rubenstien et al. 2018; Fasbender et al. 2019; Lu, Zhao and While 2019). Therefore, in line with previous research, it is hypothesized;

> *H2:*   *Employees' job satisfaction relates negatively to turnover intention.*

2.2.3 Political Skill, Job Satisfaction and Turnover Intention

A recent study of turnover intention has conceptualized and operationalized the context in four different ways, including the following: personal fit (personal similarities and differences from others), attitudinal climate (comparison of personal attitudes and behaviors with social benchmarks in the organization), the job market, and turnover contagion (motivation to quit the job when turnover rates are high in the organization) (Rubenstein et al. 2018). The research proposed a link of relations among these different contextual factors to ultimately and indirectly cause TI in the employees. Harris, Harris and Brouer (2009), verified the significant moderating role of PS on TI and JS. However, in the present study we argue that PS of an employee enables that employee to perceive the attitudinal climate as positive, thus indirectly affecting the turnover intention through enhanced job satisfaction.

When a politically skilled employee is optimistic about the work environment, TI is expected to be lower (Harris et al. 2009). Since an optimistic individual will always look for the bright side of the picture and will try to dig out and exploit the potential avenues, the idea of quitting rarely comes up. However, if the perception of a highly politically skilled employee about the environment is pessimistic, the chances of TI will be high, as that person has an astute understanding of the work environment as poor (Ferris et al. 2005), and the skill set possessed by that person will make him or her confident that finding an alternative job will be easy. Moreover, employees with high PS are proficient in developing networks and relations (Ferris et al. 2005). They are therefore expected to build connections even outside the organization, enabling them to identify more opportunities to leave their present job for another (Harris et al. 2009).

However, in the earlier hypothesis we argued that PS will have a positive effect on JS, and therefore it can be further argued that increased JS due to PS may lead to lower TI as the JS and TI relation is already well established in the literature. This leads to the next hypothesis of the study, that PS will have an indirect impact on TI through JS, where JS will play the role of a mediator. Thus, it is hypothesized that:

> *H3: Employees' job satisfaction mediates the relationship between their political skill and turnover intention.*

2.2.4 Moderating Role of POP

Several research studies have explored the moderating effects of organizational situations, such as justice and political climate, on the relationship between PS and job outcomes, but with contradictory findings (Kimura 2015). Andrews, Kacmar and Harris (2009) explained that the relationship between PS and performance is positive in high-justice environments, where the level of perceived fairness is high, and negative in low-justice environments, where the level of perceived fairness is low. A reverse situation in the case of POP can be expected because organizational justice and POP are significantly and negatively correlated (Andrews and Kacmar 2001). In contradiction to these results, Kapoutsis et al. (2011) showed that in a low POP condition i.e. where perceived politics and injustice in an organization is considered low by employees, an increase in PS leads to higher job performance, while in a high POP condition i.e. where perceived politics and injustice in organization is considered high by employees, an increase in PS has no significant effect. However, Gallagher and Laird (2008) found a significant interaction or moderating effect of political decision-making environments and PS on JS, showing that the negative effects of political decision making on JS could be reduced by a high level of PS. Conversely, Brouer et al. (2011) found insignificant interaction effects of POP and PS on JS and other individual level outcomes. These results were surprising for the researchers. These findings offer a puzzling picture that asks for an additional and more nuanced understanding of the relationship between PS and POP. Furthermore, none of these studies explored any indirect effects on TI through JS. However, Harris et al. (2009) studied the interaction effect of PS on TI and JS.

In line with Brouer et al. (2011) and Kimura (2015), it is argued that high POP environments are "weak situations" and low POP environments are "strong situations". Strong situations entail rule-based environments with little importance ascribed to personality traits such as PS (Andrews et al. 2009). Weak situations are environments where "it may not be "by the books" performance that is rewarded. It may be that the types of behaviors that are rewarded are those that go above and beyond the specific job description" (Brouer et al. 2011). Such weak situations provide extra advantage to politically skilled individuals (over low politically skilled individuals) to survive and thrive, due to their ability to adapt and manipulate such situations to their benefit.

As the literature suggests, assumption of the reality rather than the reality itself influences individuals (Lewin 1936; Ferris et al. 1989). Certain specific personal skills enable an individual to work effectively in an environment perceived as political (Ferris et al. 2005). Therefore, the long-established negative outcomes of POP may prove otherwise for different personality types possessing various diverse skills (Brouer et al. 2006). The expectancy theory (Vroom 1964), however, states that employees with high levels of expectancy associate required performance with their high levels of effort (Van and Thierry 1996). Further, instrumentality - the expectation of rewards in return for high performance, is possessed by those who have high expectancy (Van and Thierry 1996). Fudge and Schlacter (1999) state that valence is placing a high value on the provided rewards. Applying the expectancy theory (Vroom 1964), we argue that PS will act as a buffer to increase JS in perceived organizational politics. Expectancy theory is a process theory of motivation, though a number of researchers have applied it for investigating the levels of JS (Mitchell 1974). Politically skilled individuals are more able to understand and sustain themselves in a political setting (Ferris et al. 2007). They are aware of the information concerning what is expected from them, since they understand the environment well because of their social astuteness and networking skills (Brouer et al. 2011). As politically skilled individuals evaluate themselves more highly, they receive more favorable feedback from the environment through positive interpersonal effectiveness (Brouer et al. 2011). Politically skilled individuals' understanding of the environment enables them to work according to the expectations. This understanding ensures high expectancy levels of the individuals. Since they mostly have accurate information, they come up to the expectations of supervisors who recognize them as high performers. Therefore, the expectation for rewards is high. Moreover, the correct information makes them aware of the prospective rewards, which are desirable for the individual confirming valence. To further support the hypothesis, we argue that the expectancy, instrumentality and valence remains high in politically skilled individuals when POP is high, and as these individuals tend to be more satisfied in these circumstances (Brouer et al. 2011) they are less likely to leave their jobs.

Another theoretical explanation for the relationship of PS and JS in the presence of POP (political environment) can be grounded in the person-environment fit theory presented by Caplan (1987) which was initially proposed by French, Rodgers and Cobb (1974). The theory proposes that an optimum match between the personal capabilities of the employees and the work environment results in better outcomes. Since the abilities of employees are relevant and acknowledged when they are readily required at the workplace, the employees will be able to recognize their significant presence in the organization which may lead to job satisfaction. Here it can be proposed that people characterized by high PS could perceive that they have more fit in environment characterized by strong organizational politics and this better fit leads them to feel more satisfied. Thus at high level of POP the relationship between PS and JS becomes stronger.

It is therefore hypothesized;

H4a: *The positive relationship between employees' political skill and job satisfaction is moderated by perceived organizational politics, such that the relationship is stronger when POP is high.*

H4b: *The negative indirect relationship of employees' political skill on turnover intention through job satisfaction is moderated by perceived organizational politics, such that the relationship is stronger when POP is high.*

Figure 2.1

Theoretical Model on Political Skill, Organizational Politics and its Outcomes

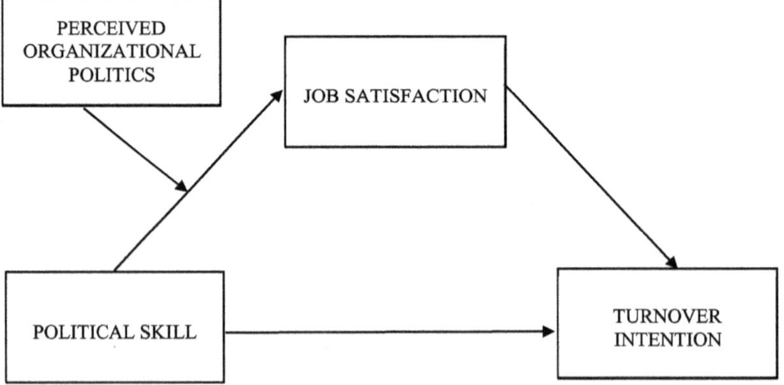

2.3 Political Skill and Abusive Supervision

2.3.1 Abusive Supervision and Political skill

Tepper (2000) first proposed the concept of abusive supervision (AS), as defined in the earlier section. Although the negative effects of the behavior may not reveal themselves immediately (Harris et al. 2013), and the outcomes may differ from one person to another as it is a subjective phenomenon (Tepper 2000), the long term effect can be seriously detrimental for the organization (Harris et al. 2013). Due to the harmful outcomes of abusive supervision including job dissatisfaction, turnover and deviance (Martinko et al. 2013), a number of researchers have shifted their focus to the predictors or antecedents of the phenomenon. The importance of this phenomenon has thus noticeably increased.

One of the important factors of leadership style not only affects the organization as a whole (Chen et al. 2015), but the position held by the supervisors enables them to have a deep impact on employee outcomes through supervisors' behaviors and practices (Li et al. 2016). AS has two dimensions, namely, active and passive abusive supervision, which in later research is also called overt and covert abusive supervision (Hutchinson 2015). Research studies have also shown that AS can be a response to certain subordinates' behavior or characteristics (Tepper et al. 2017). Ferris et al. (2005), believed that individuals with good PS are more effective in interacting with and influencing their supervisors. Recent research suggests that in return the supervisors provide better mentoring functions to such individuals (Qian et al. 2016). In the present study, PS of the subordinate with reference to its impact on AS will be investigated. The prior empirical work that combined PS and AS reported contradictory results. A meta-analysis by Zhang and Bednall (2016) reported a positive but insignificant correlation between subordinate PS and AS. In contrast, Li et al. (2016) found that PS neutralizes the effects of AS on employees' burnout. Their empirical evidence suggests that PS can be used to influence supervisors, indicating a potential buffering effect of political skill on abusive supervision. These findings offer a puzzling picture that asks for an additional and more nuanced understanding of the relationship.

Political skill acts as a guard against social stressors (Yousaf et al. 2013). One study suggested that perceived low power distance and uncertainty avoidance results in better citizenship behavior of politically skilled employees (Mahajan and Toh 2017). This, however, is dependent on the group cultural values as well (Mahajan and Toh 2017). In the present study, PS at the subordinate level was tested in a high power distance culture to investigate if such skill helped to create a positive impression that in turn reduced abusive supervision.

Mintzberg (1983) and Pfeffer (1981) explained the earliest conception of PS as a social influential behavior. The individuals proficient in PS possess positive psychological traits e.g. positive affectivity and proactivity (Ferris et al. 2008). PS plays an important role for the uplift of the employee through effective social interaction in the organization (Treadway et al. 2007). Researchers claim that social influence behavior maximizes the perception of sincerity and genuineness and hides the hidden motives of the individual (Jones 1990; Stengel 2000). Therefore, it helps employees to achieve success in their respective organizations (Harris et al. 2007) by displaying positive attitudes.

Ferris et al. (2007) explains four dimensions that constitute PS traits in an individual. These are social astuteness, interpersonal influence, apparent sincerity, and networking (Ferris et al. 2007). Recent research has explained that combining these dimensions results in enhancing the ability of the individuals to become more sensitive to the social clues and accordingly to show greater concern, resulting in the building of strong social networks (Bentley et al. 2017).

Hochwarter et al. (2006) applied the conservation of resource theory to imply that PS can efficiently and effectively work as personal resource for the employee. With the effective utilization of this personal resource, social resources can be protected efficiently (Bentley et al. 2017). Highly politically skilled employees, therefore, tend to remain more stable in unfavorable environments. Bentley et al. (2017) suggested that individuals high in political skill efficiently utilize their social astuteness in determining their short and long term behaviors to ensure maximum personal benefits in all respects. Another recent work by McAllister et al. (2016), explains the three-stage social influence process by the people who are high in political skill. As suggested, individuals will follow three stages of the process: opportunity recognition, opportunity evaluation, and opportunity capitalization (McAllister et al. 2016). As highly politically skilled individuals are more socially embedded, they encounter more opportunities to influence those around them. After deeply analyzing the opportunity, they attempt to influence the targets (Bentley et al. 2017). This process enables them to build social resources such as power, status, and reputation (Bentley et al. 2017). The proper utilization of PS by highly politically skilled individuals enables them to create a positive image, not only among their peers but also among their supervisors, which helps them to avoid abusive supervision.

The current study thus investigates the subordinates' characteristics of political skill to establish that such skill diminishes abusive supervisory behavior. It is, therefore, hypothesized as follows:

> *Hypothesis 5* Political skill of the employee impacts the abusive behavior of the supervisor such that individuals high in political skill will face less abusive supervision.

2.3.2 Moderating Effect of Gender

Ferris et al. (2007) suggested that motivation and opportunity are key determinants of use of political skill as a personal resource. It is argued that, in the context of the present study, men might have higher motivation and opportunities to use PS as a resource to avoid abusive supervision. Abusive supervision has been studied to have a different impact on males and females (Haggard et al. 2011). AS will have a greater psychological impact on females as compared to males (Haggard et al. 2011).

Empirical evidence demonstrates the difference in the levels of victimization experienced by men and women (Tepper 2007). Generally, in organizations, males are more prone to victimization as compared to the females. Even in situations of stress and work pressure, females are given leverage because of their gender (Glick and Fiske 1996). In contrast, males are considered more responsible and accountable in stressful situations. This gender specific preferential treatment is called "chivalry bias" (Visher 1983). "Its underlying assumption is that women should be treated with greater leniency and accorded more sympathetic responses than men because of their greater need for protection" (Aquino and Byron 2002, p.74). A similar pattern was observed by Khan et al. (2016), as they showed that women face less AS in comparison to men. In the context of our study, we argue that men with high PS, in comparison to women with a similar level of PS, are more likely to use their political skill as a resource to avoid abusive supervision, as they need it more because they face more harsh behavior of the supervisors. In other words, men use their PS more effectively to avoid abusive supervision as compared to women.

Since men need more resources to avoid the victimization and AS in the workplace, they generally possess a certain set of attributes that might help them to use their PS. Men tend to be more extroverted than women (Limura and Taku 2018; Lynn and Martin 1997). Blickle et al. (2010) found that the interaction between PS and extroversion has a positive association with personal performance. This observation suggests that individuals with a high level of extroversion, as opposed to a low level of extroversion, use their PS more effectively. This has led to the concept that since men are more extroverted than women in nature, they are better able to utilize their political skill in order to get the desired outcomes. Furthermore, some societies have more well-defined gender roles in contrast to others (Datta and Agarwal 2017). The context in which this study was undertaken is male dominant. Therefore, a conservative culture, like Pakistan, has a limited number of women in leadership or managerial positions (Toh and Leonardelli 2013). In line with this observation, in our sample, nearly ninety-seven percent of the supervisors are males. There is evidence that women are considered outsiders in a male dominant structure (Blass et al. 2007; Treadway et al. 2005; Knippen et al. 2019). Thus, it might be convenient for men with high PS, in comparison to women with a similar level of PS, to access their supervisors and use their political skill to influence them to get favorable treatment.

To further support the argument, social role theory can be employed, reflecting that the two genders differ from each other psychologically, which causes them to behave differently in various situations (Eagly and Wood 1999). Moreover, socially they are expected to behave in a certain way, according to the roles associated with their genders (Ouyang et al. 2015). Both role definition and the social context can influence their actions. In the Pakistani context specially, where most supervisor positions are held by males, women are confined to certain roles, thus preventing them from using their PS. The cultural setting based on Islamic values does not encourage women to socialize with their male colleagues or bosses, thus leaving them with fewer opportunities to utilize their PS for favorable outcomes. In contrast, men have the advantage of using their political skill in order to get positive outcomes or reduce negative consequences. Therefore, based on all the above arguments, it is hypothesized:

> *Hypothesis 6* Subordinates' gender will moderate the relationships between abusive supervision and political skill such that males with high political skill will face less abusive supervision.

Figure 2.2

Theoretical Model on Political Skill and Abusive Supervision

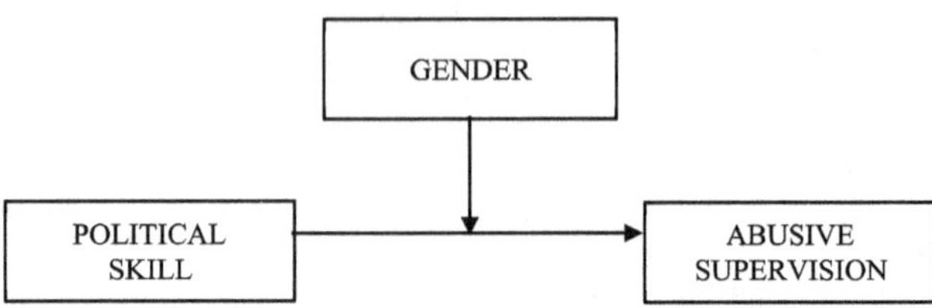

Summary

The chapter covered a general review of the literature on the study variables. First, a broad view about the politics in an organization was presented. Following that, PS was explained in detail including the construct development and dimension-wise discussion. The outcomes of political skill and pacifying effects of political skill were explored. After that, POP was discussed with a specific focus on its definition, antecedents and outcomes. Next, the literature on abusive supervision was described by defining the term and investigating the outcomes and antecedents. Subsequently, job satisfaction and turnover intention were discussed with detailed reference to the literature. Following the literature section, hypotheses were presented on the political skill and employee level outcomes. In this section the impact of PS on JS and TI was discussed and the interaction effect of POP was developed. An overall model was presented on employee level outcomes. Lastly, the impact of political skill on supervisor level outcomes was explained where political skill was postulated to reduce abusive supervision. Also, the impact of gender was developed based on theoretical assumptions. Finally, a model was presented on supervisor level outcomes.

Chapter 3

Methodology

Introduction

This chapter covers different dimensions of the methodology adopted for the study. Methodology profoundly depends upon the philosophical underpinnings of the researcher. Therefore, the first section explains the philosophical assumptions underpinning the study. Thereafter, specific research methods and techniques of the developed theoretical models are elaborated. The data description, measures and results and discussion of both models are elaborated. Next, a detailed analysis is presented to test the hypotheses developed earlier. Lastly, the limitations of the study are discussed.

3.1 Research Philosophy

Research philosophy refers to "a system of beliefs and assumptions about the development of knowledge" (Saunders et al. 2015). Well-grounded philosophical underpinning assumptions serve as a strong foundation to develop a well-structured and properly integrated research work. Philosophy specifically spells out the path to be adopted while enlarging and developing the existing knowledge. New knowledge may or may not be as sophisticated as developing a new theory, however, the solution of a current problem may also be counted as new knowledge (Saunders et al. 2015). To carry out a research process, researchers make some assumptions at different stages (Burrell and Morgan 2016). The understanding of research questions, methods and interpretation of results significantly depend upon these assumptions (Crotty 1998), which if properly and consistently chosen, establish a reliable research philosophy (Saunders et al. 2015). The ontological, epistemological and axiological are the most important philosophical underpinnings.

Ontology refers to assumptions about the nature of reality (Saunders et al. 2015). Epistemology states assumptions about knowledge, what constitutes acceptable, valid and legitimate knowledge, and how we can communicate knowledge to others (Burrell and Morgan 2016). Axiology refers to the role of values and ethics (Saunders et al. 2015).

Based on these philosophical assumptions, two schools of thought emerged as objectivism and subjectivism. Objectivism's assumptions of ontology are that there is only one true social reality experienced by all; epistemologically they discover 'the truth' about the world, through observable, measurable facts; and axiologically, objectivists try to keep their research free of values, which they believe could bias their findings (Saunders et al. 2015). On the other hand, the subjectivist's ontological belief is that everyone's reality is different, based on their social interaction and perception; epistemologically, the subjectivist researcher is interested in different opinions and narratives that can help to account for different social realities of different social actors; and axiologically, subjectivists assume that since they actively use these data, they cannot detach themselves from their own values (Saunders et al. 2015).

Burrell and Morgan (2016) proposed two dimensions on the basis of political or ideological orientation called sociology of regulation (unity and cohesiveness of society and structures) and sociology of radical change (overturning the existing state of affairs) (Saunders et al. 2015). Based on objectivism/ subjectivism and regulation/ radical change, four paradigms were proposed with different philosophical underpinning assumptions (Burrell and Morgan 2016).

The present research is grounded in a functionalist paradigm which itself is based on objectivism and sociology of regulation. Research conducted on this paradigm logically explains the relationships and suggests solutions for the structures (Saunders et al. 2015). The underlying assumption of one universal reality ensures generalized applicability of research findings in similar contexts, given accurate implementation (Kelemen and Rumens 2008).

The research philosophy used is the positivist. This will help build some concrete outcomes for establishing the results from models. The soft side of the research will, however, be compromised by this paradigm. But the nature of the research requires empirical testing. The result inferred would require a high level of reliability and validity to be implemented in practical instances. Therefore, the use of a positivist paradigm best serves the purpose.

3.2 Political Skill, Organizational Politics and its Outcomes

3.2.1 Data Description

The research approach explained in the philosophy section leads to an objective data collection method. The most commonly used tool for data collection in the social sciences is a research questionnaire. The same has been adopted in this research study. The developed constructs for the measurement of the variables were adopted from the literature. To enhance the validity and reliability of the instrument developed, a pilot survey was initially conducted. From the outcome of pilot study, the accepted instrument was then administered to the respondents.

The population of this study included all the employees of the private sector organizations currently working. The organizations from diverse sectors were chosen to enhance generalizability of the study. The sampling technique used for drawing the sample was convenience sampling. The assumption for this sampling technique is that the population elements are homogenous in nature. Therefore, the random and convenience sampling would provide similar results. Moreover, for the present study, the population was finite but unknown. There was no source to supply a reliable list of the total population elements. Therefore, in the absence of population size, a random selection for sampling was not possible.

The unit of analysis for the present study was individual, where data have been collected from employees. The study was cross sectional, meaning that data were collected without any long lag of time as in longitudinal studies. However, data were collected in two waves to avoid the common method bias (Podsakoff et al. 2003). The PS and POP were reported in the first wave along with the demographics (gender, age and qualification), while the second wave reported the level of JS and TI of the employees after a gap of two to four weeks. Moreover, researcher interference in the present research was minimal. No artificial settings were established, and instead, data were collected from the organization in the normal routine of the business.

A total number of 275 English-language based surveys were administered to the employees from different privately-owned organizations in Lahore, Pakistan. The understandability of the English language for the purpose of data collection in research is evident as a precedent from previous studies already conducted in the same region with the same language and tool used for data collection (e.g. Khan et al. 2016). Out of 275 surveys administered, 186 responses were received, yielding a response rate of 67.63%.

3.2.2 Measures

Items measured in the survey were anchored on a 5-point scale.

Political Skill

Political skill of the employees is the focal variable of the study. The study revolved around the outcomes associated with PS. Individuals possessing PS use their inherent social intelligence to apply in diverse situations in order to appear sincere and sufficiently trustworthy to influence others (Ferris et al. 2007). PS was measured using an 18-items scale developed by Ferris et al. (2005). The scale consists of four dimensions including networking ability, interpersonal influence, social astuteness and apparent sincerity. The average of these eighteen questions was taken to get the final construct. Following are the items of the construct:

1. I spend a lot of time and effort networking with others at work.

2. I can make most people feel comfortable and at ease around me.

3.   I am able to communicate easily and effectively with others.

4.   It is easy for me to develop good rapport with most people.

5.   I understand people well.

6.   I am good at building relationships with influential people at work.

7.   I am particularly good at sensing the motivations and hidden agendas of others.

8.   When communicating with others, I try to be genuine in what I say and do.

9.   I have developed a large network of colleagues and associates at work whom I can call on for support when I really need to get things done.

10.   At work, I know a lot of important people and am well connected.

11.   I spend a lot of time and effort developing connections with others at work.

12.   I am good at getting people to like me.

13.   It is important that people believe I am sincere in what I say and do.

14.   I try to show a genuine interest in other people.

15.   I am good at using my connections and networks to make things happen at work.

16.   I have good intuition or savvy about how to present myself to others.

17.   I always seem to instinctively know the right things to say or do to influence others.

18.   I pay close attention to people's facial expressions.

Perceived Organizational Politics

Perception of organizational politics is a very crucial phenomenon in the literature as it has been associated with a number of deleterious outcomes. POP was measured using a 12-items scale developed by Kacmar and Ferris (1991). The following 12 questions were asked to ascertain the POP of the employees;

1.   One group always gets their way.

2.   There are influential groups no one crosses.

3.   Policy changes help only a few.

4.   People build themselves up by tearing others down.

5.   Favoritism not merit gets people ahead.

6.   Employees don't speak up for fear of retaliation.

7.   Promotion goes to top performers.

8.   Rewards come to hard workers.

9.   Employees are encouraged to speak out.

10.   No place for yes men.

11.   Pay and promotion policies are not politically applied.

12.   Pay and promotion decisions are consistent with policies.

Job Satisfaction

Job satisfaction is an important workplace outcome. JS of the employees was measured using a 6-items shorter version of Brayfield and Rothe's (1951) 18-items scale, developed and used by Agho, Price and Mueller (1992). The average of the six items was calculated to determine the final construct. Following are the items of the construct:

1.   I find real enjoyment in my job.

2.   I like my job better than the average person.

3.   I am seldom bored with my job.

4.   I would not consider taking another kind of job.

5.   Most days I am enthusiastic about my job.

6.   I feel fairly well satisfied with my job.

Turnover Intention

Turnover intention is a very deleterious phenomenon in the organization. TI of the employees was measured using a 3-items scale by Micheals and Spector (1982). The reliability of the construct is $\alpha = 0.92$. Following are the items of the construct:

1.   I often seriously think about quitting my organization.

2.   I want to quit my organization.

3.   I am actually planning to quit my organization.

Control Variables

The variables were controlled that could have possibly affected the postulated relationships. Most of the studies in social research tend to control the demographic variables to avoid their potential impact of the relationship. As the literature suggests, gender, age and qualification of the employees were controlled (De Clercq et al. 2018).

3.2.3 Results and Discussion

Descriptive Analysis
In this section the demographic variables of the study are elaborated. The table below represents the frequencies and percentages of the demographics. The majority of the respondents were males representing 78.5% of the total sample. This represents major participation of males in industry. The major age group represented in the sample was in between 25 to 30 years of age. In addition, 50% of the respondents held bachelors degrees. Organizations for data collection came primarily from heavy engineering (machinery, automobiles, and motorcycles etc.), service industry (software, banking, and telecom etc.), agriculture, and paper and packaging industries. Almost 55% of the respondents were from the service industry, while 45% were from heavy engineering, agriculture and paper and packaging.

Table 3.1

Demographic Information

	Frequency	Percentage
Gender		
Male	146	78.5
Female	40	21.5
Age		
Less than 25 years	21	11.3
25-30 years	89	47.8
31-34 years	49	26.3
35-40 years	20	10.8
41-44 years	2	1.1
45-50 years	2	1.1
51-54 years	3	1.6
Qualification		
Intermediate	4	2.2
Bachelors	93	50
Masters	86	46.2
M.Phil	3	1.6

Note. $N = 186$.

The table below represents the descriptive statistics of the study variables, including the control variables. From the mean values the inclination of the response can be evaluated. Standard deviation, maximum and minimum values are also mentioned in the table.

Table 3.2

Descriptive Statistics

	Mean	Standard Deviation	Maximum	Minimum
Gender	.22	.41	1.00	.00
Age	2.52	1.10	7.00	1.00
Qualification	2.47	.57	4.00	1.00
Political Skill	3.67	.52	5.00	2.06
Perceived Organizational Politics	2.86	.62	4.83	1.00
Job Satisfaction	3.32	.62	5.00	1.17
Turnover Intention	2.57	1.09	5.00	1.00

Note. $N = 186$.

Correlation Analysis

Correlation among the variables defines the association of one variable with the other, indicating how much change in one variable is caused by a change in another variable. The table below describes the correlation of the variables of the study. PS is significantly positively related to JS and significantly negatively related to TI. POP is significantly negatively related to JS. JS and TI are also significantly negatively related.

Table 3.3

Correlation Analysis

	1	2	3	4	5	6	7
1. Gender	-						
2. Age	-.20**	-					
3. Qualification	.19*	.10	-				
4. Political Skill	.12	-.004	.04	-			
5. Perceived Organizational Politics	-.02	.19**	.10	-.13	-		
6. Job Satisfaction	.02	-.04	.05	.22**	-.27**	-	
7. Turnover Intention	.02	.03	-.08	-.15*	.14	-.45**	-

Note. $N = 186$.
$^*p < .05$. $^{**}p < .01$ (two-tailed tests).

Reliability

Heale and Twycross (2015) explained reliability as the extent of the accuracy and consistency of a given measurement tool in quantitative research. Ideally, the results extracted by the tool should be consistent over the period of time in similar conditions. Reliability of the instrument can be assessed on the basis of three attributes, namely; homogeneity, stability and equivalence (Heale and Twycross 2015). In order to check the reliability of the constructs, Kimberlin and Winterstein (2008) claimed Cronbach's alpha as the most widely used technique. It is the average of the inter-correlations of the items of the constructs and number of items in the scale (Kimberlin and Winterstein 2008; Hair et al. 2006). The acceptable value of Cronbach's alpha ranges from 0.6 to 0.7. However, values above 0.7 are considered good for assessing the reliability of the construct (Hair et al. 2006).

The table below presents the Cronbach's alpha value of the constructs of the study. The reliability value of PS with 18 items construct is 0.9, which is well above 0.7. Hence the reliability of this scale is ensured. POP also demonstrates 0.79 value of Cronbach's alpha reliability, which also shows a good value within the acceptable range. JS, composed of 6 items, showed 0.74 reliability value, which is a good fit. Lastly, TI with 3 items scale has a reliability of 0.92, which is also a good fit.

Table 3.4

Cronbach's Alpha Reliability

Sr. No.	Constructs	No. of Items	Cronbach's Alpha Value
1.	Political Skill	18	0.90
2.	Perceived Organizational Politics	12	0.79
3.	Job Satisfaction	06	0.74
4.	Turnover Intention	03	0.92

Common Method Bias

Most management and organization-related research utilizes the questionnaire survey technique to collect data for the measurement of independent and dependent variables (Tehseen, Ramayah and Sajilan 2017). However, common method variance (CMV) bias, which is the systematic variance shared among the variables, may enhance the bias risk among variables (Jakobsen and Jensen 2015). CMV had been defined as the systematic error variance that is shared among variables that are measured with the same source or method (Richardson, Simmering and Sturman 2009). This in turn can bias the estimated relationships among variables or measures (Campbell and Fiske 1959). The estimated relationships can be either inflated or deflated in the prevalence of CMV (Jakobsen and Jensen 2015). CMV shows a false correlation among the variables of study because of the utilization of one method of measurement (Tehseen et al. 2017). Additionally, CMV is a threat to the validity of the relationships of the study (Reio 2010). Also, the generalizability of the results is doubtful in the presence of CMV (Yüksel 2017)

The common sources of common method variance are single item context, respondent, measurement context and item characteristics. (Reio 2010). Thus, CMV must be checked for self-reported questionnaires, especially when both predictor and criterion variables are reported by a single source (Podsakoff et al. 2003). Chang et al. (2010) identified four sources of CMV which are: (i) measurement of dependent and independent variables from the same respondent; (ii) item presentation; (iii) context of presentation of items in the questionnaire; (iv) and the contextual affects. Generally, two approaches can be employed to control CMV including careful procedure design and statistical methods to control the CMV impact after data collection (Podaskoff et al. 2012). Procedural controls are usually employed before data collection (Tehseen et al. 2017), which include, collecting data on dependent and independent variables from different sources, protecting anonymity of the respondents, counterbalancing the sequence of predictor and criterion measurement, improving items through careful construction of variables and sequential, psychological or methodological separation of dependent and independent variables (Podaskoff et al. 2003). The separation of the variables is, however, possible by placing a time lag in the measurement of criterion and predictor variables, providing a cover letter to clarify the distinct purpose of measurement, stating diverse situations to the respondents, and using different question formats (Tehseen et al. 2017). Although the procedural remedies can be applied before data collection, occasionally the application of these remedies is not possible in all circumstances (Tehseen et al. 2017). Therefore, statistical techniques may be used to check and avoid CMV. The most common techniques include: (a) Harman's Single-Factor Test, (b) Partial Correlation Procedures, (c) Correlation Matrix Procedure, and (d) The Measured Latent Marker Variable Approach.

Since the literature acknowledges the eminent issue of common method bias, especially in organizational research (Tehseen, Ramayah and Sajilan 2017), the present research fully addresses the concern by utilizing the statistical test and controls.

In order to overcome the common method bias, the methodological approach of two wave data collection was adopted. However, the unmeasured latent methods factor test (Podsakoff et al. 2012) was performed to check for any potential impact of common method bias. A common method factor was introduced that included all principal constructs' indicators. The degree to which each indicator's variance was then explained by its principal construct, and common method variance factor was calculated. According to the results, all method factor loadings were insignificant, and the indicators' substantive variances were substantially higher than the method variances. The ratio of substantive variance to method variance was about 247:1. Therefore, common method bias was not a significant issue with regard to our data.

Confirmatory Factor Analysis
The degree to which a concept is exactly measured in a quantitative study is referred to as validity (Heale and Twycross 2015). In other words, a construct should measure what it says it will measure. For example, if a tool is expected to measure POP it should be measuring the same and not any other concept related to politics or any other topic. Three types of validity including content validity (tool covers all the contents of the variable), construct validity (inferences can be drawn from the test scores) and criterion validity (comparison with other construct measuring same variable) have been explained in the literature (Heale and Twycross 2015). Different tools are available for measuring the validity of the construct. In this research, confirmatory factor analysis has been conducted to confirm the validity of the instrument.

The underlying purpose of conducting a test to check the validity of a construct is to ensure that the latent variable is presenting a separate and distinct construct. In order to conform to the assumption, for the purpose of analysis, confirmatory factor analysis was conducted using AMOS. The present study used constructs with a large number of items representing the same construct. Judge et al. (2002) argued that variables with a large number of items explaining the specific construct can have an adverse effect on the model fit. The values may get disturbed in the presence of a large number of factor loadings given the large number of items. To address the issue, the variables with numerous items were divided into parcels. Parceling involves making subsets of the items of the construct, then taking the average of each subset to be used as an individual item for factor loading. The subsets can be made on the basis of any similarity (e.g. dimensions) and correlation or without any specific parameter. In this study, PS is represented by 18 items and POP is represented by 12 items. Recent research on PS also applied parceling for analyzing constructs with a large number of items (Smith and Webster 2017). Therefore, for the construct of PS we divided the items into 4 parcels according to the dimensions (Smith and Webster 2017), while for POP the items were divided into 4 parcels containing 3 items in each parcel using a heterogeneous assignment (Cole, Perkins and Zelkowitz 2016).

Measurement Model

To assess the model fit in confirmatory factor analysis (CFA), we used the Chi-square statistic, Root Mean Square Error of Approximation (RMSEA; acceptable fit: 0.05–0.08), the Standardized Root Mean Square Residual (SRMR; acceptable fit: 0.05–0.10, good fit: 0–0.05), the Comparative Fit Index (CFI; acceptable fit: 0.90–97, good fit: 0.97–1) and the Tucker-Lewis Index (TLI; acceptable fit: greater than 0.90) (Bentler 1990; Hu and Bentler 1999; Schermelleh-Engel, Moosbrugger and Muller 2003; Marsh, Hau and Wen 2004; Chen et al. 2008; Bentler and Bonett 1980). The results of CFA supported the proposed 4-factor model, (χ^2 (113) = 192.907, RMSEA = 0.06, SRMR = 0.05, CFI = 0.942, TLI = 0.930). The same model was tested on items converged into different combinations, but the model fit was worse than the 4-factor model. For example, when items of four constructs converged into one factor, the result was a very poor model fit (χ^2 (209) = 5.35, p= 0.000, RMSEA = 0.153, SRMR = 0.092, CFI = 0.493, TLI = 0.440). Moreover, in the 4-factor model, all the items loaded significantly on their respective factors. The average variance extracted (AVE) for all the factors is 0.5 or above exhibiting convergent validity. AVE is greater than the squared correlations with other factors. These results established the convergent and discriminant validity of our model.

Hypothesis Testing

The table below (Table 3.5) shows the results of regression using simple linear regression and Process Macro in SPSS by Hayes (2013). Model 1 in the table shows the impact of control variables on job satisfaction. To test the first hypothesis, Model 2 in the table shows a significant relationship between PS and JS. According to the results, our first hypothesis is supported confirming the positive relation of PS and JS. To assess the second hypothesis, Model 4 from the table indicates the significant impact of JS on turnover intention. Hence, the second hypothesis is supported.

Table 3.5

Regression Analysis

	Job Satisfaction			Turnover Intention
	Model 1	**Model 2**	**Model 3**	**Model 4**
Gender	-.001	-.036	-.040	.155
Age	-.026	-.003	-.008	.031
Qualification	.058	.077	.088	-.142
Political skill		.227**	.233**	-.122
Perceived Organizational Politics		-.253**	-.270***	
Political skill x POP			.295*	
Job Satisfaction				-.757***
R^2	0.004	0.112	0.133	0.215
ΔR^2		0.108	0.021	

Notes: n=186.
(+ p < .10) (* p < .05) (** p < .01) (*** p < .001)

To test the mediation in the third hypothesis, Model 4 of Process Macro by Hayes (2013) was run for simple mediation. The confidence interval for the indirect effect of PS on TI through JS does not include zero (-0.39, -0.05). Thus, the third hypothesis of the study is supported.

Table 3.6

Mediation Analysis

Political Skill	Turnover Intention		
	B	**SE**	**CI**
Total effect	-.32	.15	(-.62, -.02)
Direct effect	-.12	.14	(-.40, .16)
Indirect effect	-.20	.08	(-.39, -.05)

To test the moderated mediation, Model 7 of Process Macro was used. In order to test the moderating effect of perceived organizational politics, the interaction term (political skill x perceived organizational politics) is calculated in Model 3 in Table 3.5. The interaction term is significant in supporting the hypothesis 4a. Moreover, the impact of PS on JS at high and low levels of perceived organizational politics is plotted in Figure 3.1. The graph indicates that PS may enhance the JS of the employees where organizational politics is perceived as higher.

Figure 3.1

The Moderating Effect of POP on Political Skill and Job Satisfaction

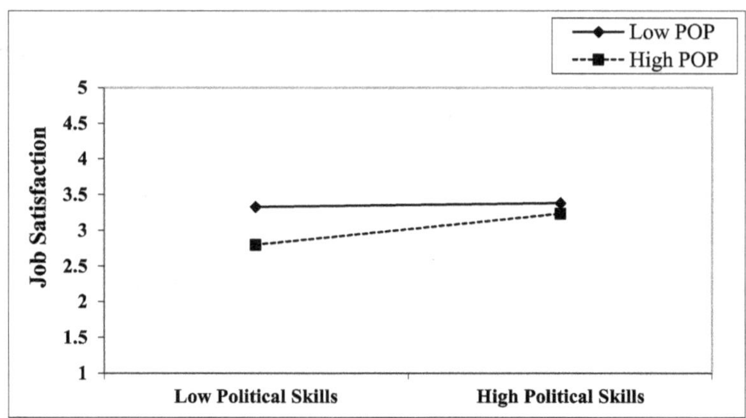

Lastly, to check the conditional indirect effect of PS on TI of the employees, perceived organizational politics was investigated at three levels i.e. -1 SD, M, +1 SD. Table 3.7 exhibits the results of indirect effects. The conditional indirect effects of PS on employees' turnover intentions become insignificant (including zero) at a lower level (-1 SD) of perceived organizational politics (B = -.04, 95% CI [-.27, .21]). However, this effect becomes significant (i.e. different from zero) at a higher level (+1 SD) of perceived organizational politics (B = -.32, 95% CI [-.58, -.10]). Therefore, hypothesis 4b is supported.

Table 3.7

Indirect Effects of Political Skill on Employee Turnover Intention via Job Satisfaction at Low, Mean and High Levels of Perceived Organizational Politics

	Indirect Effect	Boot SE	95% Bias-Corrected Confidence Interval	
			Lower	Upper
Low Perceived Organizational Politics	-.04	.12	-.27	.21
Mean Perceived Organizational Politics	-.18	.08	-.35	-.04
High Perceived Organizational Politics	-.32	.12	-.58	-.10

3.3   Political Skill and Abusive Supervision

3.3.1 Data Description

For the purpose of data collection, the questionnaire method has been adopted in this research study. The constructs developed for the measurement of the variables were adopted from the literature. To enhance the validity and reliability of the instrument developed, a pilot survey was initially conducted. From the outcome of pilot study, the accepted instrument was then administered to the respondents.

Initially, the supervisor and subordinate dyads were matched from the list of subordinates under each supervisor in various organizations. Maximum two to five subordinates under each supervisor were selected to avoid data nesting issue. After matching the dyads, the data were collected in two waves. In the first wave, data from the supervisor were collected. Along with that the data on the independent variables from the subordinates were collected. After a time lag of two to three weeks in the second wave, the data on the dependent variables were collected from the subordinates.

The population of this study included all the employees of the private sector organizations currently working. The organizations from diverse sectors were chosen to enhance the generalizability of the study. The sampling technique used for drawing the sample was convenience sampling. The assumption for this sampling technique is that the population elements are homogenous in nature. Therefore, random and convenience sampling would provide similar results. For the present study, the population was finite but unknown. There was no available source that offered a reliable list of the total population elements. Therefore, in the absence of population size, random selection of the sample was not possible.

The unit of analysis for the present study was individual, where data were collected from employees. The study was cross sectional, meaning that data were collected without any long lag of time as in longitudinal studies. Researcher interference in the present research was minimal. No artificial settings were established, but rather, data were collected from the organization in the normal routine of the business.

A total number of 275 English-language based surveys were administered to the subordinates and their respective supervisors from different privately owned organizations in Pakistan. Out of 275 surveys administered, 178 subordinate – supervisor dyad responses were received, making a response rate of 64.72%. Almost 59% of the respondents were from service industry and 41% were from Heavy Engineering, Agriculture and Paper and Packaging.

3.3.2 Measures

Items measured in the survey were anchored on a 5-point scale, except for subordinate performance.

Subordinate perceptions of abusive supervision
To measure abusive supervision, the 15-item scale developed by Tepper (2000) was used. The score on all 15 questions was averaged out to construct a total score for abusive supervision. The subordinates were asked about the frequency of such supervisory behaviors as:

1.   My boss ridicules me.

2.   My boss tells me my thoughts or feelings are stupid.

3.   My boss gives me the silent treatment.

4.   My boss puts me down in front of others.

5.   My boss invades my privacy.

6.   My boss reminds me of my past mistakes and failures.

7.   My boss doesn't give me credit for jobs requiring a lot of effort.

8.   My boss blames me to save himself/herself embarrassment.

9.   My boss breaks promises he/she makes.

10.   My boss expresses anger at me when he/she is mad for another reason.

11.   My boss makes negative comments about me to others.

12.   My boss is rude to me.

13.   My boss does not allow me to interact with my coworkers.

14.   My boss tells me I am incompetent.

15.   My boss lies to me.

Political skill

Political skill of the employees was measured using the 18-items scale developed by Ferris et al. (2005). The average of these eighteen questions was found in order to determine the final construct. The construct items are listed in the earlier section.

Control variables

The variables were controlled that could have possibly affected the postulated relationships. As the literature suggested, subordinates' gender, subordinates' age, supervisors' gender and supervisors' organizational tenure were controlled (Khan et al. 2016). In addition, the performance of the subordinate as evaluated by the supervisor and subordinate qualification, was also controlled. To measure performance of the subordinate, the four-item scale developed by Liden, Wayne and Stilwell (1993) was used. Items were rated on different scales according to the statement of the item of the construct. Items include:

1.   Rate the overall level of performance that you observe for this subordinate.

2.   What is your personal view of this subordinate in terms of his or her overall effectiveness?

3.   Overall, to what extent do you feel this subordinate has been effectively fulfilling his or her roles and responsibilities?

4.   My subordinate is superior to other subordinates that I've supervised before.

3.3.3 Results and Discussion

Descriptive Analysis
In this section the demographic variables of the study are elaborated. The table below represents the frequencies and percentages of the demographics. The majority of the subordinates were males, comprising 75.8 of the total respondents. The respondents predominantly belonged to the age group of 25 to 30 years of age. Most of the respondents held bachelors degree. The tenure of most of the subordinates under the current supervisor was from 1 to 2 years. Supervisors were also predominantly males comprising 96.6%. Most of the supervisors have experience of 6 to 10 years.

Table 3.8

Demographic Information

	Frequency	Percent
Subordinates' Gender		
Male	135	75.8
Female	43	24.2
Subordinates' Age		
Less than 25 years	23	12.9
25-30 years	82	46.1
31-34 years	48	27
35-40 years	19	10.7
41-44 years	1	0.6
45-50 years	2	1.1
51-54 years	3	1.7
Subordinates' Qualification		
Intermediate	4	2.2
Bachelors	89	50
Masters	82	46.1
M.Phil	3	1.7
Tenure (Subordinate)		
Less than a year	61	34.3
1-2 years	78	43.8
3-5 years	26	14.6
6-10 years	11	6.2
More than 10 years	2	1.1
Supervisors' Gender		
Male	172	96.6
Female	6	3.4
Supervisors' Experience		
Less than 5 years	27	15.2
6-10 years	58	32.6
11-15 years	48	27
More than 15 years	45	25.3

Note. N = 178.

To further highlight the descriptive analysis, the table below presents the mean, standard deviation, maximum and minimum values of the study variables.

Table 3.9

Descriptive Statistics

	Mean	Standard Deviation	Maximum	Minimum
Subordinates' Gender	0.24	0.43	.00	1.00
Subordinates' Age	2.50	1.11	7.00	1.00
Subordinates' Qualification	2.47	.57	4.00	1.00
Tenure (Subordinate)	1.96	.92	5.00	1.00
Supervisors' Gender	.034	.18	1.00	.00
Supervisors' Experience	2.62	1.02	4.00	1.00
Subordinates' Performance	3.72	.72	5.00	1.5
Political Skill	3.67	.52	5.00	2.06
Abusive Supervision	1.59	.77	4.93	1

Note. N = 178.

Correlation Analysis

The correlation analysis depicts the association among variables. From the table below we see that PS is strongly negatively related to abusive supervision. Also, abusive supervision is significantly negatively related to gender.

Table 3.10

Correlation Analysis

	1	2	3	4	5	6	7	8	9
1. Subordinates' Gender	-								
2. Subordinates' Age	-.23**	-							
3. Subordinates' Qualification	.18*	.08	-						
4. Tenure (Subordinate)	-.23**	.29**	-.01	-					
5. Supervisors' Gender	.04	.00	-.04	.08	-				
6. Supervisors' Experience	-.07	.14	.10	.05	.01	-			
7. Subordinates' Performance	.01	.03	.13	.02	-.01	-.09	-		
8. Political Skill	.14	-.02	.04	-.11	.08	.04	.01	-	
9. Abusive Supervision	-.21**	-.06	.11	.04	-.03	-.06	-.14	-.23**	-

Note. $N = 178$.

*$p < .05$. **$p < .01$ (two-tailed tests).

Reliability

Heale and Twycross (2015) explained reliability as the extent of accuracy and consistency of the measurement tool used in quantitative research. This means that the results extracted by the tool should be consistent over a given period of time under similar conditions. Reliability of the instrument can be assessed on the basis of three attributes, namely homogeneity, stability and equivalence (Heale and Twycross 2015). In order to check the reliability of the constructs, Kimberlin and Winterstein (2008) claimed Cronbach's alpha as the most widely used technique. It is the average of the inter-correlations of the items of the constructs and number of items in the scale (Kimberlin and Winterstein 2008; Hair et al. 2006). The acceptable value of Cronbach's alpha ranges from 0.6 to 0.7; however, values above 0.7 are considered good for assessing the reliability of the construct (Hair et al. 2006).

The table below presents the Cronbach's alpha value of the constructs of the study. The reliability value of PS with an 18-items construct is 0.89, which is well above 0.7, hence the reliability of this scale is ensured. Abusive supervision also demonstrates a 0.93 value of Cronbach's alpha reliability, which also shows a good value within the acceptable range. Subordinates' performance, composed of 4 items, showed 0.82 reliability value, which is a good fit.

Table 3.11

Cronbach's Alpha Reliability

Sr. No.	Constructs	No. of Items	Cronbach's Alpha Value
1.	Subordinates' Performance	04	0.82
2.	Political Skill	18	0.89
3.	Abusive Supervision	15	0.93

Confirmatory Factor Analysis

Validity is the degree to which a concept is exactly measured in a quantitative study (Heale and Twycross 2015). In other words, a construct should measure what it says it will measure. For example, if a tool is expected to measure perceived organizational politics, it should be measuring the same and not any other concept related to politics. Three types of validity including content validity (tool covers all the contents of the variable), construct validity (inferences can be drawn from the test scores) and criterion validity (comparison with other construct measuring same variable) have been explained in the literature (Heale and Twycross 2015). Different tools are available for measuring the validity of the construct. In this research, confirmatory factor analysis has been conducted to confirm the validity of the instrument.

In order to conform to the assumption that each of the latent variables is presenting a separate and distinct construct, for the purpose of analysis, confirmatory factor analysis is conducted using AMOS. Judge et al. (2002), stated that a variable with a large number of items or factors explaining the specific construct can cause an adverse effect on the model fit. To address the issue of inflated measurement errors in the current study, the variables with numerous items were divided into parcels. Abusive supervision is represented by 15 items and political skill is represented by 18 items. For the construct of abusive supervision we divided the items into 5 parcels with 3 items in each parcel using heterogeneous assignment (Cole et al. 2016), and for political skill the items were divided into 4 parcels according to the four dimensions i.e. social astuteness, networking ability, interpersonal influence and apparent sincerity (Smith and Webster 2017).

To assess the model fit in confirmatory factor analysis, we used the Chi-square statistic, Root Mean Square Error of Approximation (RMSEA; acceptable fit: 0.05–0.08), the Standardized Root Mean Square Residual (SRMR; acceptable fit: 0.05–0.10, good fit: 0–0.05), the Comparative Fit Index (CFI; acceptable fit: 0.90–97, good fit: 0.97–1) and the Tucker-Lewis Index (TLI; acceptable fit: greater than 0.90) (Bentler, 1990; Hu and Bentler 1999; Schermelleh-Engel et al. 2003; Marsh et al. 2004; Chen et al. 2008; Bentler and Bonett 1980).

Model Fit

The results generated supported the proposed 3-factor model, (χ^2 (62) = 130.121, RMSEA = 0.08, SRMR = 0.043, CFI = 0.944, TLI = 0.930). . Moreover, all the items loaded significantly on their respective factors. The average variance extracted (AVE) for all the factors is 0.5 or above, exhibiting convergent validity. The same model was tested converging the items into two factors in three different combinations; the model fit was worse than the 3-factor model. The first two-factor model showed model fit values as (χ^2 (64) = 417.695, p= 0.000, RMSEA = 0.180, SRMR = 0.112, CFI = 0.711, TLI = 0.648), when abusive supervision and performance (control variable) were loaded together. The second two-factor model showed model fit values as (χ^2 (64) = 410.613, p= 0.000, RMSEA = 0.178, SRMR = 0.064, CFI = 0.717, TLI = 0.655), when abusive supervision and political skill were loaded together. Whereas, the third two-factor model showed model fit values as (χ^2 (64) = 458.781, p= 0.000, RMSEA = 0.190, SRMR = 0.088, CFI = 0.677, TLI = 0.607), when political skill and performance (control variable) were loaded together. The items when converged into one factor generated results of (χ^2 (65) = 698.085, p= 0.000, RMSEA = 0.239, SRMR = 0.122, CFI = 0.483, TLI = 0.379), which shows a very poor model fit. These results establish the convergent and discriminant validity of our model and show the absence of common method bias.

Hypothesis Testing

The table below (Table 3.2) shows the results of linear regression and moderation using the Hayes (2013) Process Macro in SPSS for moderation analysis. Model 1 in the table shows the impact of control variables on the dependent variable i.e. abusive supervision. Subordinate gender has a significantly negative impact on abusive supervision, such that males are assigned code 0 and females 1. Moreover, subordinate qualification has a significantly positive impact on abusive supervision. Here, we can take the stance of Khan et al. (2016) that a supervisor may feel threatened from a subordinate applying the social dominance orientation theory and hence become abusive with even a highly qualified subordinate. Subordinate performance has a significantly negative impact on abusive supervision, which conforms to the previous research (Tepper et al. 2011; Khan et al. 2016). Model 2 in the table introduces the independent variable in the linear regression model. To verify the first hypothesis, political skill (β = -.297, p < 0.01) is significantly negatively related to abusive supervision. Hence, our first claim is confirmed, that highly politically skilled individuals tend to reduce abusive supervision by using their political and social astuteness.

Table 3.12

Moderation Analysis

	Abusive Supervision		
	Model 1	**Model 2**	**Model 3**
Subordinate Gender	-.492**	-.446**	-.489**
Subordinate Age	-.091	-.087	-.081
Subordinate Qualification	.277**	.280**	.305**
Supervisor Gender	-.078	-.006	.109
Supervisor Experience	-.079	-.070	-.064
Subordinate Performance	-.183*	-.179*	-.186*
Tenure of the Subordinate	.021	.004	-.009
Political skill		-.297**	-.343**
Political skill*Subordinate Gender			.467*
F-Statistic	3.294**	3.978***	4.062***
R^2	.119	.158	.179
ΔR^2		.039	.021

Notes: n=178. *p < .05. **p < .01. ***p < .001

The second hypothesis is tested using the Hayes (2013) moderation analysis, using PROCESS Macro, specifically model 1. We took the mean centered variables for moderation analysis. The results show that the interplay of political skill and gender of the subordinate has a significant impact on abusive supervision. To verify the second hypothesis, Model 3 in Table 3.2 shows that interaction of gender and political skill. Hence, H_2 for the current study is also accepted. Gender plays an important moderating role on the relationship between political skill and abusive supervision since ($\beta = .467$, $p < 0.01$), such that males are coded 0 and females 1. This supports our argument that males better use the political skill to avoid abusive supervision as compared to females.

Figure 3.2 explains the role of gender in altering the relationship of political skill and abusive supervision. Women, whether high in political skill or low, face the same level of abusive supervision. Men, on the contrary, use their political skill more favorably by reducing the abusive supervision.

Figure 3.2

The Moderating Effect of Gender on Political Skill and Abusive Supervision

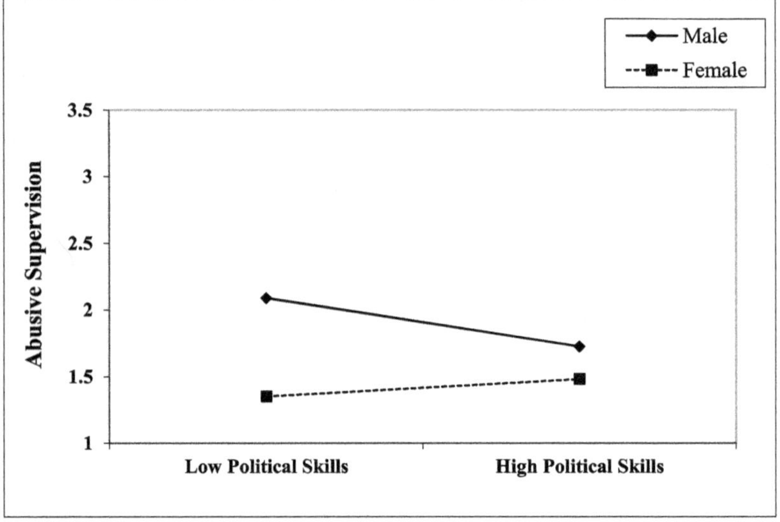

3.4   Study Limitations

The current research dissertation provides insightful perceptions about political skill. The outcomes generated from political skill in this study add theoretically and practically to the phenomenon. Along with the contributions of the research, some limitations of the study are required to be acknowledged for an honest depiction. The limitations of the study are discussed below.

3.4.1 Generalizability

The study was conducted on a limited group of people drawn from the vast target population. Since the population size was very large, it was not possible to collect the data from each element of the population. Moreover, almost every research study in the social sciences domain resorts to sample statistics to generalize the results as a population parameter. In other words, due to the enormity of the population, a sample as a representative of the whole population is used to determine population characteristics. These results are acceptable and applicable to the whole population. The study also assumed the same rationale, although this inherent limitation was unavoidable due to the time limitation, resource limitation and inability to access all the elements of the population.

Furthermore, the research was conducted in a specific geographical area of Pakistan. The data collected and the results drawn are influenced by the particular cultural and social values of this region. As also explained in the hypothesis development section, the cultural differences do influence the hypothesized relationships. The relationship proved significant and true in one culture may not show any significance in a different culture. Though it is a limitation that the study outcomes may not be applicable to various cultural settings, it is nevertheless a contribution to the literature in terms of explaining the cultural influences of various factors and associations.

3.4.2 Cross Sectional Data Collection

The data for the investigation of supervisor related outcomes were collected in a single wave i.e. data on dependent and independent variables were collected in a one-time shot. However, data for employee related outcomes were collected in two waves, where independent and moderating variables were investigated in a one-time shot, and mediating and dependent variables were asked in the second-time shot with a lag of two to three weeks. However, the procedural techniques may not prove sufficient to avoid common method bias inherent in cross section data collection. Therefore, potential common method bias may exist. This, however, was tested for by applying the relevant tests for checking the bias. Furthermore, significant interaction suggests that common method bias was not an issue. Though different models were run on AMOS to ensure model fit, future studies may incorporate longitudinal data collection for such studies. The descriptive statistics (low correlations among study variables) also revealed that common method bias was not a problem in our study. In addition, because common method variance is itself a type of main effect or correlated error, it cannot explain the moderating effects of team processes on relationship conflict (Harrison et al. 1996).

3.4.3 Convenience Sampling

The sampling technique used for the study was convenience sampling, a type of non-probability sampling where respondents are chosen on the basis of availability, proximity and willingness to respond. The major drawback of this type of sampling technique is that all the elements of the population do not have an equal chance of representation in the sample. Moreover, since the targets are chosen on a convenience basis, the representation may get skewed or include outliers. However, there are few justifications for using this sampling technique in this specific study. First, the population size was both finite and unknown. This means that although there was a finite number of respondents included in the population size, the total number of potential respondents was not known. Second, there was no record or database available to formulate a list of respondents for conducting any type of probability sampling. Lastly, the respondents were selected on the basis of availability. Finally, the researcher made sure that the respondents were capable enough to understand the questions and willing to respond to those questions.

3.4.4 Response Bias

Another limitation inherent in questionnaire-based data collection is response bias. Potentially two factors cause the bias, namely perception of the respondent about the question asked and social desirability. The constructs used in the study were developed for subjective feelings, emotions and attitudes. Though development of the constructs went through very rigor processes to ensure their validity and reliability, the perception about the question asked may still differ from one person to another. Since the subjective feelings and emotions are measured objectively, there is a fair chance of perceptional bias in understanding the phenomenon asked. To overcome this bias, a cover letter was provided to explain the purpose of the study and the anonymity of the responses. The second issue of social desirability means that the respondent may not respond honestly in order to provide a personal opinion as close to the social acceptability criteria as possible. This bias is very common when the respondent has a fear of data disclosure. To avoid this, a cover letter was attached to ensure the confidentiality of the data. Moreover, the data collection process was personally administered and responses were taken back in sealed envelopes to ensure the respondents' data safety.

3.4.5 Lack of Subjective Evaluation of Respondents

The data for this particular study were collected about the personal feelings, emotions, skills, perceptions and attitudes. However, feelings and emotions are difficult to measure. In order to objectify them, a little subjective assessment may be compromised. To minimize the issue pertaining to this limitation, already developed constructs were used to avoid any misleading outcomes. The constructs used were developed and frequently used in similar research studies, which ensures their strength.

3.4.6 Same Source Data

The data were collected from the same source for both independent and dependent variables which restricts a clear conclusion about the causality relationships. The data of study on the supervisor related outcomes were collected from a single source except for the control variable of performance. However, statistical tests ensuring the strength of the relationships and results were applied to avoid any misleading conclusions.

3.4.7 Unequal Male to Female Ratio

In the study on PS and AS, the male to female respondent ratio of the subordinates was not equal. Gender was taken as a moderating variable in the model, but equal participation of both genders would have improved the confidence level of the study. However, this is an inherent limitation due to a significant labor force participation difference in the ratio of male to female employees in Pakistan. The report of Pakistan Bureau of Statistics (2018) indicated that 48 out of 100 males, as opposed to 14 out of 100 females, participate in the total labor force, which reflects the difference in the ratio. Due to this natural characteristic of the cultural settings, a fair, if not equal, representation of both genders was attempted.

3.4.8 Low Response Rate

A total number of 275 questionnaires were administered for the data collection purposes. However, as the data were collected in two waves and dyads, it was not possible to attain a very good response rate. Thus, it is a limitation of the study.

Summary

In nutshell, the chapter covered all the methodological aspects of the study. The positivist philosophical underpinning assumptions provided the basis for the research. The epistemological, ontological and axiological assumptions were discussed. Further, the data of both the studies were discussed with respect to the sampling, unit of analysis, time horizon and researcher interference. Descriptive analysis comprising the frequencies, percentages, mean and standard deviation were explained. After that, correlation analysis was presented in detail where correlation among the variables was explained. Following that, the tests for validity and reliability were discussed in which confirmatory factor analysis and reliability analysis was done. After determining the model fit, analysis was run to test the hypothesis. Process Macro in SPSS developed by Hayes (2013) was used for mediation and moderation analysis. Based on the final analysis, all the hypotheses were accepted and discussed. Lastly, the limitations of the study were described.

Chapter 4

Conclusion and Future Research Directions

Introduction

This chapter presents a detailed discussion of the results drawn from the analysis related to the hypotheses developed in the earlier section. It covers the theoretical implications of each research study and explains its contribution in the literature. At the end, practical implications of both studies are highlighted, followed by a discussion of the utilization of the tested model and its outcomes in real world/ practice. Future research directions to extend the work in same area are then proposed for each study.

4.1 Political Skill, Organizational Politics and its Outcomes

The current study acknowledged the importance of political skill (PS) of employees by extending the pre-established models and testing them in new settings. The aim of the study was to establish a link between different individual outcomes at the employee level. Since PS has been treated as a resource in many studies (Karatepe et al. 2019; Zhao et al. 2013), the rationale of the hypothesis presented on the relationship between PS and JS is also the same. PS is a resource that is used by employees to enable a more accurate perception of the job characteristics which ultimately results in enhanced levels of job satisfaction. JS as an emotional state results in many positive outcomes. Vast literature on the positive outcomes and consequences of JS is available depicting the importance of this phenomenon in organizations. Relying on the basis provided in the literature, this research study establishes a positive link between PS and JS.

Since current literature has already discussed the positive association between PS and JS, the present study answers the call (Munyon et al. 2015) to explore its impact on turnover intention. In this research, the PS of the employees was explored for its potential impact on turnover intention through JS, which is an underexplored area in PS literature. A number of theoretical lenses help to establish the impact of job satisfaction on turnover intention (March and Simon 1958), and the present research is also based on the theoretically drawn relation. Therefore, the position has been taken that as a resource, PS will help to develop better job satisfaction which in turn helps to reduce negative outcomes in the organization in the form of lower turnover intention.

Moreover, the moderating role of perceived organization politics has been investigated as a source of positive influence on the pre-established relationship of PS and JS, applying expectancy theory by Vroom (1964). Employees with good PS will know exactly what is expected from them and will exert their effort in the right direction even in an uncertain environment. The reasoning for this interaction effect is postulated in the hypothesis development section. However, POP is expected to provide a conducive environment to politically skilled individuals to maximize their trait. This relationship was already explored in the literature (Brouer et al. 2011); however, the relationship was not judged to be significant. Therefore, the need for investigation pertained.

The analysis showed a positive relationship between PS and JS, confirming the already established associations in the literature. Further, JS mediates the relation between PS and TI such that high politically skilled individuals tend to show higher levels of JS as compared to low politically skilled individuals. Also, employees with high JS have lower TI. Further, the results show that POP moderates the relationship between PS and JS such that highly PS individuals in POP show better JS levels. Moreover, a moderated mediation prevails among the variables of the study such that POP moderated the relationship between PS and JS which further affects TI.

4.1.1 Theoretical Implications

Theoretically, the research contributes to the literature in various ways. First, the research findings are consistent with the previous research. The proposed hypothesis determining the relationship between PS and JS indicated a significantly positive relationship, as proved in the literature (Kolodinsky et al. 2004). Most of the studies were undertaken in western cultures. The influence of cultural values and norms affect the relationships developed. Since the present study is conducted in a different culture, where norms and values are defined differently (as explained in the literature section), the insights are presented from a different perspective. Theoretically it can be said that PS is positively linked with JS in the western and Pakistani culture alike.

Furthermore, our study verified that JS leads to lower TI. Our study substantiated full mediation between PS and TI through JS. This is an interesting addition to the literature, as it extends the link further to minimize the turnover intention of the employees. PS has been studied to pose an impact on JS (Kolodinsky et al. 2004), yet the present study extends it to ultimately verifying its indirect impact on reducing TI in the employees. Since turnover intention is a detrimental phenomenon in organizations, the present study aids in developing a better understanding of how to reduce TI.

The present study also provides a new insight to the literature by proving a significant moderation between POP, PS and JS. This, conversely, was not proved significant as hypothesized in a previous study (Brouer et al. 2011). The plausible factors supporting the relationship might be more prevalent in the present set up of the study to verify a significant relation. As discussed earlier, the cultural norms and organizational values in different societies affect the behavioral outcomes. Drawing on the same rationale, the present study settings provide better context to explore the relation hypothesized. This contribution to the literature will enable the researchers to understand the contextual factors affecting the tested relationship.

4.1.2 Practical Implications

The findings of the current study have practical implications for the organizations specially operating in the cultural settings of a developing country such as Pakistan. As hypothesized, the study showed a significantly positive relation between PS and JS. PS not only brings about positive consequences but as the study shows, it also helps reduce negative behaviors such as TI through JS. This result implies the importance to employees in the organizations of acquiring good PS. Therefore, keeping in mind the importance of PS, organizations may make an extra effort to provide training to their employees to acquire such skills.

In addition, the employees themselves can take the initiative to learn PS for better survival in the organization. As the research findings have highlighted the importance of learning PS as a positive resource for successful survival even in uncertain conditions, employees will acknowledge the importance of learning this skill. The uncertainty or politics in any organizational set up are nearly impossible to reduce or avoid due to their penetration of the structure. Even if an effort is made to minimize the level of politics in an organization, it will take a very long time to realize any definitive outcome. In such a situation, the negative impact of politics on employees can be reduced by taking appropriate measures and responding early. Therefore, such skills (like PS) could reduce some negative effects of political environment in organizations.

Organizations are often perceived as political by the employees. POP has been shown to have a negative impact on the performance and behavioral outcomes of employees. The present study makes an important contribution in this respect by proving that PS enables JS for the employees in a political environment. Therefore, managers may overcome the negative outcomes of a political environment through enabling the employees to acquire PS through effective development programs for enhancing such skills.

4.2 Political Skill and Abusive Supervision

Grounded in the conservation of resource theory, the argument was established that political skill will act as a resource for the employees to buffer the abusive behavior of a supervisor. The concept developed enables an understanding of the dual functionality of political skill. Firstly, high political skill individuals will be better able to show positive outcomes, as suggested in the earlier literature. Secondly, political skill will help in avoiding negative outcomes. From the data collected by the employees in the present study, the results drawn support the argument developed. The results show a significantly negative relation between political skill and abusive supervision.

The present research followed the earlier idea by Hochwarter et al. (2006) of treating political skill as a resource. Results show that in reality, individuals with high political skill exploit the trait by avoiding negative leadership behavior. As discussed earlier, the person high in political skill will be better able to find an opportunity to influence others (Bentley et al. 2017). Since finding the right opportunity helps to build a positive image, high politically skilled individuals leave a positive impression on the supervisor as well. The rationale is in line with the findings of Treadway et al. (2007), where high PS resulted in better impression management. The favorable rating of the individual by the supervisor results in low abusive behavior. Extracting from the literature, this finding is also in the similar direction of the previous research where dark triad individuals with high PS were able to get favorable ratings from their supervisors, resulting in better performance ratings (Templer 2018).

The current study further investigated the moderating role of gender on the already established relationship of political skill and abusive supervision. Drawing on the assumptions in the hypothesis development, males were expected to be more proficient in using their political skill to avoid unfavorable supervisor behaviors. The analysis supported the position presented. According to the results, males with high PS avoid abusive supervision. The findings of research through the interaction effect of political skill and gender also show an interesting insight where high political skill in females has been linked with increased abusive supervision. This outcome reveals that since females have not been given equality in the contextual settings of Pakistan, even good political skill does not let them gain practical advantages in the workplace. The findings of the research thus indicate that at management level the issue needs to be addressed where the supervision must be evaluated carefully to eliminate providing inherent advantages to males on the basis of gender. Females must be treated fairly and impartially to enable them achieve maximum benefits regardless of the gender. Normally, such behaviors and attitudes are considered taboo and bring defamation to the person involved. However, being a male dominant society, no such hindrance comes in the way of males to exercise political skill. Therefore, males with high PS demonstrated the actual utility and benefit of its application.

However, the interaction effect of political skill and gender shows contradictory results for both the genders. Males with high political skill face less abusive supervision, whereas females with high political skill face more abusive supervision. As discussed earlier, females are considered to conform to the roles defined by the contextual settings (Ouyang et al., 2015). Pakistan has as a tight culture, where societal norms are strongly held and any deviation in their execution may result in severe sanctions (Gelfand et al., 2011; Triandis, 1989). In culturally tight countries, women are more likely to conform to gender roles defined by the society and any deviation may not be tolerated, resulting in greater use of penalties for women who do choose to deviate from the expected norm (Gelfand et al., 2011; Toh and Leonardelli, 2012). Political behavior is not an expected conduct from females. Therefore, females with high political skill may be considered in violation of the standards set by the society. As a response, the supervisor may consider it offensive and react by increased abusive behavior.

4.2.1 Theoretical Implications

The findings of the study are consistent with the earlier conducted research. Our study shows that political skill helps to reduce the negative impact/ behaviors in the workplace, specifically abusive supervision. This finding is in line with the earlier research by Zhou et al. (2015), which explains that political skill reduces the negative impact of workplace aggression. However, they treated the four dimensions of political skill as moderator separately. In the present study, political skill as a collective construct composed of the four dimensions was taken as an independent variable for explaining reduced abusive behavior from the supervisor.

Furthermore, gender plays an important role in altering the impact of abusive supervision such that highly politically skilled males are likely to face less abusive supervision. However, for females, political skill does not alter much of the already sustained abusive behavior, as they face more abusive supervision. The arguments used for establishing the relationship explain the plausible reasons for the relationship. However currently, certain perspectives, particularly for the study settings and respondents, are able to explain the reasons for the developed relationship, as presented earlier. From earlier research, Ferris et al. (2012) stated that extraversion is linked with political skill such that extroverts are better able to utilize their political skill due to their high networking ability. In the present study settings, males in particular are more extroverted. The social role theory (Eagly and Wood 1999) explains the role definition of different players in the society. Moreover, Lynn and Martin (1997) in their study conducted in 37 countries, confirmed that in general, males are more extroverted than females. Our study, therefore, is consistent with the findings in the earlier research that males being more extroverted better utilize their political skill to avoid abusive supervision.

Since the study setting has a high-power distance culture with a prevalence of abusive supervision, it provides a good context for a study on abusive supervision (Khan et al., 2016). In a conservative and male dominated culture, like Pakistan, women might be considered outsiders. Thus, it might be convenient for men with high political skill, in comparison to women with similar level of political skill, to access and impress their supervisors using their social astuteness, interpersonal influence, apparent sincerity and networking skills (Ferris et al., 2007) to avoid abusive behavior.

The study augments the literature on political skill and abusive supervision. Since political skill is beneficial for individual growth, the current study helps to support that it also reduces the impact of negative behaviors in organizations. It explains how politically enabled individuals minimize the impact of abusive supervision. Further, the study helps to explain the role of gender in the organizations. It will enlighten managers in practice to deliberately treat both genders equally in certain situations.

4.2.2 Practical Implications

The findings of the current study have practical implications for organizations specially operating in the cultural settings of a developing country such as Pakistan. As hypothesized, the study showed a significantly negative relation between political skill and abusive supervision. Political skill not only brings about positive consequences, but as the study shows, it also helps to reduce negative behaviors such as abusive supervision.

This implies the importance of acquiring good political skill for the employees in the organizations. Therefore, keeping in view the importance of political skill, organizations may make an extra effort to provide training for their employees to acquire such skills. Hence, some negative behaviors and outcomes in organizations may be reduced.

Organizations maintain a diverse workforce with respect to gender, age, and race etc. The managers have to deal with a variety of diverse situations. The current study clearly reveals bias in dealing with the different genders. The concept of in-group and out-group presented in the literature has been verified in the study where females are treated as the out-group in a male dominant culture. Therefore, the management must take into account the issue pertaining to this occurrence by enabling females to contribute more to organizational performance. As a suggestion, some common interest areas can be introduced in the organizations where females can participate and be treated as an in-group without any gender bias.

Further, the difference in use and utility of political skill with different genders is also evident. Men take more advantage of their political skill as compared to women because organizations are male dominant, especially in the context of our study. Females might get limited opportunities to access their supervisors and managers to exhibit political skill. Women are at a disadvantage in comparison to men. The managers, therefore, can make an effort to create an inclusive environment for both the genders. Consequently, females may also be able to utilize and benefit from their political skill.

Nevertheless to realistically overcome the gender bias, a thorough cultural transformation and multilevel support is inevitable. Syed and Ali (2019) advocated a "process" approach which focuses on cultural level initiation for change instead of a "reform" approach which aggressively imposes values, to reduce gender inequality. Specifically with reference to Pakistan, where macro level issues including economy, labor force participation, literacy, religion, law and culture contribute to gender inequality (Syed and Ali, 2019), numerous efforts at governmental level are already in place to reduce imbalance. However, the impact of these efforts is not much felt in the absence of a "process" oriented approach (Syed and Ali, 2019). Based on the same rationale, we suggest that organizations must initiate gradual change process from policy level to overcome gender bias. The importance of diversified workforce with justified female participation must be acknowledged during the policy making process and allocation of rewards and benefits. Furthermore, professional trainings can be arranged for management and employees regarding gender sensitivities, roles, responsibilities, attitudes and behaviors. This initiative will have dual impact, where managers will be well-informed about their role in bridging the gap as well as females will also be well-aware of their rights and privileges. Besides, women particularly need to lift themselves up in order to take their due rights. Professionally, they can develop strategies to negotiate on major issues for a progressive participation in the workforce. Also, strategies for proficient enhancement of their job related skills must be developed. Such initiatives may prove helpful in overcoming the inherent gender bias in organizations.

4.3   Future Research Directions

Though political skill has been investigated to positively affect favorable employee outcomes and negatively affect adverse employee outcomes, various factors are yet to be explored. Such factors may include, though are not limited to, organizational commitment, knowledge sharing, innovation and readiness for change. Organizations these days are in need of finding out the skills and traits possessed by employees that result in positive organizational performance. Therefore, research in this direction will be helpful from a practical perspective as well.

Furthermore, the linkages or associations of PS with positive outcomes through different mediating or moderating factors will provide interesting avenues for investigation. Since a proven path will be helpful in explaining the anticipated outcomes, the practical implication of such research will be dual. Through explaining the mediating and moderating factors, the strength of PS and its relationship with other factors can be thoroughly explained. An important path of PS to reduced turnover intention can be through embeddedness since employee will feel more embedded in the workplace due to PS, which will lead to lower motivation to switch the job. It can be an important variable to be researched in the future studies.

Another interesting area of research with respect to perceived organizational politics can be explored by identifying such skills, traits or factors that help to bring positive results in high POP environment. POP has always been linked with causing adverse outcomes in organizations. However, following the rationale presented in this study, certain personal or external factors may indicate a more effective use of POP to ensure positive outcomes. Future studies must explore such factors to encourage positive outcomes even in political environments.

As has been explained earlier, while the interaction of POP and PS has shown insignificant results in an earlier study, the current study has presented a significant relationship. The conflicting results have been explained due to the differences in the situational and contextual conditions of the research. To generalize the findings, POP can be explored in other cultural settings for its potential impact on employee outcomes with the interaction of various employee traits and skills. The contrast in research findings calls for meaningful research in the same direction, undertaking the contextual and other demographic variables affecting the relationship.

The present research also confirms the claims it established that political skill significantly reduces the abusive behavior of supervisors. Moreover, gender plays a vital role in determining the strength of this relationship. In order to continue meaningful research in the same direction, other demographic variables can be used, such as employee age, qualification, experience etc. as well as supervisor age, gender, experience as moderators. Since demographics as moderators are not yet common in the research, the impact of such factors is very significant in shaping the behavioral outcomes of people. Specifically, the relationship of supervisor and subordinate is influenced by many factors including demographics. If the boss and employee belong to the same place or region, it is most possible that the relationship will be influenced by this factor. Moreover, older employees are usually at an advantage from a young supervisor, as the age factor restricts the supervisor being abusive or harsh with subordinates. However, all these assumptions are as yet not discussed in the literature. This provides significant room for research which will offer deep insights to the literature.

Moreover, political skill can also be researched further to reduce the negative outcomes pertaining in the organizations, thereby making it more obvious that positive use of political skill can be helpful for organizations. PS has been immensely recognized as a pacifying factor in negative situations. The research can provide a broad array of deleterious factors that can be avoided by using the PS of employees.

Furthermore, gap between the practice and the law exists in societies like Pakistan, where women are generally treated irrespective of the legislature (Syed and Ali, 2019). Therefore, a future study in this direction will provide insights to overcome such issues.

Abusive supervision can be investigated to determine the influence of certain other personal traits. Since abusive supervision has been acknowledged as a deleterious organizational phenomenon, more research focus should be shifted to discovering the factors that help to avoid it. The present study has successfully established the link between PS and abusive supervision such that high PS individuals face less abusive supervision. The underlying rationale was the utilization of PS as a resource. Additional research focusing on other factors, which can be used as resources, can provide insightful avenues for expanding the work in abusive supervision literature. A number of personal skills, traits and attitudes of employees can be investigated to potentially influence abusive supervision. Furthermore, a large sample study would be more insightful as the present study has this limitation. Also cross-cultural study on the gender roles would provide variant perceptions.

Summary

Overall, the study contributes to the political skill literature at two levels. First, political skill with reference to employee-level outcomes, including job satisfaction and turnover intention, was explored. Specifically, the results have drawn attention to the importance of PS in a political environment. The study has made an additional contribution by providing empirical evidence for the interplay of POP in the already established relationship between PS and JS. Lastly, political skill in relation to supervisor-level outcome i.e. abusive supervision in organizations, was emphasized. Specifically, the results highlighted the importance of political skill in an abusive supervisory environment. The study has made an additional contribution by providing empirical evidence for the interplay of gender in the already established negative relationship between political skill and abusive supervision. Therefore, the study has made a significant contribution towards theory and practice.

References

Abbas, M., & Raja, U. (2014). Impact of perceived organizational politics on supervisory-rated innovative performance and job stress: Evidence from Pakistan. *Journal of Advanced Management Science*, 2(2), 158-162.

Addae, H.M., Praveen Parboteeah, K., & Davis, E.E. (2006). Organizational commitment and intentions to quit: An examination of the moderating effects of psychological contract breach in Trinidad and Tobago. *International Journal of Organizational Analysis*, 14(3), 225-238.

Agho, A. O., Price, J. L., & Mueller, C. W. (1992). Discriminant validity of measures of job satisfaction, positive affectivity and negative affectivity. Journal of occupational and organizational psychology, 65(3), 185-195.

Ahearn, K. K., Ferris, G. R., Hochwarter, W. A., Douglas, C., & Ammeter, A. P. (2004). Leader political skill and team performance. *Journal of Management*, 30(3), 309-327.

Akirmak, U., & Ayla, P. (2019). How is time perspective related to burnout and job satisfaction? A conservation of resources perspective. *Personality and Individual Differences*. doi: 10.1016/j.paid.2019.109667

Alegre, I., Mas-Machuca, M., & Berbegal-Mirabent, J. (2016). Antecedents of employee job satisfaction: Do they matter? *Journal of Business Research*, 69(4), 1390-1395.

Ali, F., & Syed, J. (2017). From rhetoric to reality: A multilevel analysis of gender equality in Pakistani organizations. *Gender, Work & Organization*, 24(5), 472-486.

Andrews, M. C., & Kacmar, K. M. (2001). Discriminating among organizational politics, justice, and support. *Journal of Organizational Behavior: The International Journal of Industrial, Occupational and Organizational Psychology and Behavior*, 22(4), 347-366. doi: 10.1002/job.92

Andrews, M. C., Kacmar, K. M., & Harris, K. J. (2009). Got political skill? The impact of justice on the importance of political skill for job performance. *Journal of Applied Psychology*, 94(6), 1427-37.

Aquino, K., & Byron, K. (2002). Dominating interpersonal behavior and perceived victimization in groups: Evidence for a curvilinear relationship. *Journal of Management*, 28, 69-87.

Aquino, K., & Thau, S. (2009). Workplace victimization: Aggression from the target's perspective. *Annual Review of Psychology*, 60, 717-41.

Aryee, S., Sun, L. Y., Chen, Z. X. G., & Debrah, Y. A. (2008). Abusive supervision and contextual performance: The mediating role of emotional exhaustion and the moderating role of work unit structure. *Management and Organization Review*, 4(3), 393-411.

Aryee, S., Chen, Z. X., & Budhwar, P. S. (2004). Exchange fairness and employee performance: An examination of the relationship between organizational politics and procedural justice. *Organizational behavior and human decision processes*, 94(1), 1-14.

Atwater, L., Kim, K. Y., Witt, A., Latheef, Z., Callison, K., Elkins, T. J., & Zheng, D. (2016). Reactions to abusive supervision: Examining the roles of emotions and gender in the USA. *The International Journal of Human Resource Management*, 27(16), 1874-1899.

Aryee, S., Chen, Z. X., Sun, L., & Debrah, Y. (2007). Antecedents and outcomes of abusive supervision in Chinese setting. *Journal of Applied Psychology*, 92, 191-201.

Bakker, A. B., & Demerouti, E. (2007). The job demands-resources model: State of the art. *Journal of Managerial Psychology*, 22, 309-28.

Baloch, M. A., Meng, F., Xu, Z., Cepeda-Carrion, I., & Bari, M. W. (2017). Dark triad, perceptions of organizational politics and counterproductive work behaviors: The moderating effect of political skills. *Frontiers in Psychology*, doi: 10.3389/fpsyg. 2017.01972

Bandura A. (1973). *Aggression: A Social Learning Analysis*. Englewood Cliffs, NJ: Prentice Hall.

Banister, C. M., & Meriac, J. P. (2015). Political skill and work attitudes: A comparison of multiple social effectiveness constructs. *The Journal of Psychology*, 149(8), 775-795.

Barnes, C. M., Lucianetti, L., Bhave, D. P., & Christian, M. S. (2015). You wouldn't like me when I'm sleepy: Leaders' sleep, daily abusive supervision, and work unit engagement. *Academy of Management Journal*, 58(5), 1419-1437.

Barreiro, P. L., & Albandoz, J. P. (2001). Population and sample. Sampling techniques. *Management Mathematics for European Schools*, 1(1), 1-18.

Baumeister, R. F., Vohs, K. D., & Tice, D. M. (2007). The strength model of self-control. *Current Directions in Psychological Science*, 16(6), 351-355.

Bennett, R. J., Deen, C., Harvey, P., Leonard, S. R., Li, Y., Mackey, J., Martinko, M. J., Ocampo, A. C., Parker, S. L., Posey, C., & Restubog, S. L. D. (2018). Abusive supervision: Causes and consequences. In *Academy of Management Proceedings*, 2018(1), 12757). Briarcliff Manor, NY 10510: Academy of Management. doi: 10.5465/AMBPP.2018.12757symposium

Bentler, P. M. (1990). Comparative fit indexes in structural models. *Psychological Bulletin*, 107(2), 238-246.

Bentler, P. M., & Bonett, D. G. (1980). Significance tests and goodness of fit in the analysis of covariance structures. *Psychological Bulletin*, 88(3), 588-606.

Bentley, J. R., Treadway, D. C., Williams, L. V., Gazdag, B. A., & Yang, J. (2017). The moderating effect of employee political skill on the link between perceptions of a victimizing work environment and job performance. *Frontiers in Psychology*, 8, 850.

Bertelli, A. M. (2007). Determinants of bureaucratic turnover intention: Evidence from the Department of the Treasury. *Journal of Public Administration Research and Theory*, 17(2), 235-258.

Bing, M. N., Davison, H. K., Minor, I., Novicevic, M. M., & Frink, D. D. (2011). The prediction of task and contextual performance by political skill: A meta-analysis and moderator test. *Journal of Vocational Behavior*, 79(2), 563-577.

Blass, F. R., Brouer, R. L., Perrewé, P. L., & Ferris, G. R. (2007). Politics understanding and networking ability as a function of mentoring: The roles of gender and race. *Journal of Leadership & Organizational Studies*, 14(2), 93-105.

Blickle, G., Ferris, G. R., Munyon, T. P., Momm, T., Zettler, I., Schneider, P. B., & Buckley, M. R. (2011). A multi-source, multi-study investigation of job performance prediction by political skill. *Applied Psychology*, 60(3), 449-474.

Blickle, G., Wendel, S., & Ferris, G. R. (2010). Political skill as moderator of personality–job performance relationships in socioanalytic theory: Test of the getting ahead motive in automobile sales. *Journal of Vocational Behavior*, 76(2), 326-335.

Bluedorn, A. C. (1982). A unified model of turnover from organizations. *Human Relations*, 35(2), 135-153.

Bortolon, C., Lopes, B., Capdevielle, D., Macioce, V., & Raffard, S. (2019). The roles of cognitive avoidance, rumination and negative affect in the association between abusive supervision in the workplace and non-clinical paranoia in a sample of workers working in France. *Psychiatry Research*, 271, 581-589.

Brayfield, A. H., & Rothe, H. F. (1951). An index of job satisfaction. *Journal of Applied Psychology*, 35(5), 307-311.

Brees, J., Mackey, J., Martinko, M., & Harvey, P. (2014). The mediating role of perceptions of abusive supervision in the relationship between personality and aggression. *Journal of Leadership & Organizational Studies,* 21(4), 403-413.

Brouer, R. L., Ferris, G. R., Hochwarter, W. A., Laird, M. D., & Gilmore, D. C. (2006). The strain-related reactions to perceptions of organizational politics as a workplace stressor: Political skill as a neutralizer. *Handbook of Organizational Politics*, 187, 206. Edward Elgar Publishing, Inc, Northampton, MA.

Brouer, R. L., Harris, K. J., & Kacmar, K. M. (2011). The moderating effects of political skill on the perceived politics–outcome relationships. *Journal of Organizational Behavior*, 32(6), 869-885.

Brown, M. E., Treviño, L. K., & Harrison, D. A. (2005). Ethical leadership: A social learning perspective for construct development and testing. *Organizational Behavior and Human Decision Processes*, 97(2), 117-134.

Brown, T. A., & Moore, M. T. (2012). Confirmatory factor analysis. *Handbook of structural equation modeling*, 361-379.

Burić, I., & Moe, A. (2020). What makes teachers enthusiastic: The interplay of positive affect, self-efficacy and job satisfaction? *Teaching and Teacher Education*, 89, 103008.

Burrell, G., & Morgan, G. (2016). *Sociological Paradigms and Organisational Analysis*. Abingdon: Routledge (originally published by Heinemann 1979).

Cahyono, E., Haryono, T., Haryanto, B., & Harsono, M. (2020). The role of gender in the relationship between abusive supervision and employee's organisational citizenship behaviour in Indonesia. *International Journal of Trade and Global Markets*, 13(3), 311-322.

Campbell, D. T., & Fiske, D. W. (1959). Convergent and discriminant validation by the multitrait-multimethod matrix. *Psychological bulletin*, 56(2), 81-105.

Caplan, R.D. (1987). Person-environment fit theory and organizations: Commensurate dimensions, time perspectives, and mechanisms. *Journal of Vocational behavior*, 31(3), 248-267.

Carlson, D. S., Ferguson, M., Perrewé, P. L., & Whitten, D. (2011). The fallout from abusive supervision: An examination of subordinates and their partners. *Personnel Psychology*, 64(4), 937-961.

Carlson, D., Ferguson, M., Hunter, E., & Whitten, D. (2012). Abusive supervision and work–family conflict: The path through emotional labor and burnout. *The Leadership Quarterly*, 23(5), 849-859.

Carver, C. S. (1979). A cybernetic model of self-attention processes. *Journal of Personality and Social Psychology*, 37(8), 1251-81.

Carver, C. S., & Scheier, M. F. (1982). Control theory: A useful conceptual framework for personality–social, clinical, and health psychology. *Psychological Bulletin*, 92(1), 111-35.

Chan, M. E., & McAllister, D. J. (2014). Abusive supervision through the lens of employee state paranoia. *Academy of Management Review*, 39(1), 44-66.

Chang, C. H., Rosen, C. C., & Levy, P. E. (2009). The relationship between perceptions of organizational politics and employee attitudes, strain, and behavior: A meta-analytic examination. *Academy of Management Journal*, 52(4), 779-801.

Chang, S. J., Van Witteloostuijn, A., & Eden, L. (2010). From the editors: Common method variance in international business research. *Journal of International Business Studies*, 41(2), 178-84.

Chen, F., Curran, P. J., Bollen, K. A., Kirby, J., & Paxton, P. (2008). An empirical evaluation of the use of fixed cutoff points in RMSEA test statistic in structural equation models. *Sociological Methods & Research*, 36(4), 462-494.

Chen, Z., Zhu, J., & Zhou, M. (2015). How does a servant leader fuel the service fire? A multilevel model of servant leadership, individual self identity, group competition climate, and customer service performance. *Journal of Applied Psychology*, 100(2), 511-21.

Cho, H. T., & Yang, J. S. (2018). How perceptions of organizational politics influence self-determined motivation: The mediating role of work mood. *Asia Pacific Management Review*, 23(1), 60-69.

Chukwuorji, J. C., Uzuegbu, C. N., Agbo, F., Ifeagwazi, C. M., & Ebulum, G. C. (2020). Different slopes for different folks: Gender moderates the relationship between empathy and narcissism. *Current Psychology*, 39, 1808-1818

Clements, J. A., Boyle, R., & Proudfoot, J. G. (2016). Exploring political skill and deception. *International Journal of Sociology and Social Policy*, 36(¾), 138-56.

Cole, D. A., Perkins, C. E., & Zelkowitz, R. L. (2016). Impact of homogeneous and heterogeneous parceling strategies when latent variables represent multidimensional constructs. *Psychological Methods*, 21(2), 164-74.

Conway, N., & Coyle-Shapiro, J. A. M. (2012). The reciprocal relationship between psychological contract fulfilment and employee performance and the moderating role of perceived organizational support and tenure. *Journal of occupational and Organizational Psychology*, 85(2), 277-299.

Courtright, S. H., Gardner, R. G., Smith, T. A., McCormick, B. W., & Colbert, A. E. (2016). My family made me do it: A cross-domain, self-regulatory perspective on antecedents to abusive supervision. *Academy of Management Journal*, 59(5), 1630-1652.

Crotty, M. (1998). *The Foundations of Social Research*. London: Sage.

Dai, Y. D., Zhuang, W. L., & Huan, T. C. (2019). Engage or quit? The moderating role of abusive supervision between resilience, intention to leave and work engagement. *Tourism Management*, 70, 69-77.

Datta, S., & Agarwal, U. A. (2017). Factors effecting career advancement of Indian women managers. *South Asian Journal of Business Studies*, 6(3), 314-36.

De Clercq, D., Haq, I. U., Azeem, M. U., & Raja, U. (2018). Family incivility, emotional exhaustion at work, and being a good soldier: The buffering roles of waypower and willpower. *Journal of Business Research*, 89, 27-36.

Deci, E. L., and Ryan, R. M. (2002). *Handbook of self-determination research*. University Rochester Press, New York, NY.

Demerouti, E., Bakker, A. B., Nachreiner, F., & Schaufeli, W. B. (2001). The job demands-resources model of burnout. *Journal of Applied Psychology*, 86(3), 499-512.

Dickter, D. N., Roznowski, M., & Harrison, D. A. (1996). Temporal tempering: An event history analysis of the process of voluntary turnover. *Journal of Applied Psychology*, 81(6), 705-16.

Dollard, J., Miller, N. E., Doob, L. W., Mowrer, O. H., & Sears, R. R. (1939). *Frustration and aggression.* Yale University Press, New Haven, CT.

Dormann, C., & Zapf, D. (2001). Job satisfaction: A meta-analysis of stabilities. *Journal of Organizational Behavior: The International Journal of Industrial, Occupational and Organizational Psychology and Behavior*, 22(5), 483-504.

Drory, A. (1993). Perceived political climate and job attitudes. *Organization Studies*, 14(1), 59-71.

Duffy, M. K., Ganster, D. C., & Pagon, M. (2002). Social undermining in the workplace. *Academy of management Journal*, 45(2), 331-351.

Dunnette, M.D., & Locke, E.A. (1976). The Nature and Causes of Job Satisfaction. *Handbook of Industrial and Organizational Psychology.* Rand McNally College Publishing Company Chicago.

Eagly, A. H. (1987). *Sex differences in social behavior: A social-role interpretation,* Hillsdale: Erlbaum.

Eagly, A. H. (1997). Sex differences in social behavior: comparing social role theory and evolutionary psychology. *American Psychologist*, 52(12), 1380-1383.

Eagly, A. H., & Wood, W. (1999). The origins of sex differences in human behavior: Evolved dispositions versus social roles. *American psychologist*, 54(6), 408-23.

Egan, T. M., Yang, B., & Bartlett, K. R. (2004). The effects of organizational learning culture and job satisfaction on motivation to transfer learning and turnover intention. *Human Resource Development Quarterly*, 15(3), 279-301.

Etikan, I., Musa, S. A., & Alkassim, R. S. (2016). Comparison of convenience sampling and purposive sampling. *American Journal of Theoretical and Applied Statistics*, 5(1), 1-4.

Falbe, C. M., & Yukl, G. (1992). Consequences for managers of using single influence tactics and combinations of tactics. *Academy of Management Journal*, 35(3), 638-652.

Fasbender, U., Van der Heijden, B. I., & Grimshaw, S. (2019). Job satisfaction, job stress and nurses' turnover intentions: The moderating roles of on-the-job and off-the-job embeddedness. *Journal of Advanced Nursing*, 75(2), 327-337.

Ferris, D. L., Johnson, R. E., Rosen, C. C., Djurdjevic, E., Chang, C. H. D., & Tan, J. A. (2013). When is success not satisfying? Integrating regulatory focus and approach/avoidance motivation theories to explain the relation between core self-evaluation and job satisfaction. *Journal of Applied Psychology*, 98(2), 342-53.

Ferris, G. R., & Kacmar, K. M. (1992). Perceptions of organizational politics. *Journal of Management*, 18(1), 93-116.

Ferris, G. R., & Judge, T. A. (1991). Personnel/human resources management: A political influence perspective. *Journal of Management*, 17(2), 447-488.

Ferris, G. R., & King, T. R. (1991). Politics in human resources decisions: A walk on the dark side. *Organizational Dynamics*, 20(2), 59-71.

Ferris, G. R., & Mitchell, T. R. (1987). The components of social influence and their importance for human resources research. *Research in Personnel and Human Resources Management*, 5, 103-128.

Ferris, G. R., Treadway, D. C., Perrewé, P. L., Brouer, R. L., Douglas, C., & Lux, S. (2007). Political skill in organizations. *Journal of Management*, 33(3), 290-320.

Ferris, G. R., Treadway, D. C., Kolodinsky, R. W., Hochwarter, W. A., Kacmar, C. J., Douglas, C., & Frink, D. D. (2005). Development and validation of the political skill inventory. *Journal of Management*, 31(1), 126-152.

Ferris, G. R., Frink, D. D., & Galang, M. C. (1993). Diversity in the Workplace: The Human Resources Management Challenges. *Human Resource Planning*, 16(1), 41-51.

Ferris, G.R., Blickle, G., Schneider, P.B., Kramer, J., Zettler, I., Solga, J., Noethen, D., & Meurs, J.A. (2008). Political skill construct and criterion-related validation: a two-study investigation. *Journal of Managerial Psychology*, 23(7), 744-71.

Ferris, G. R., Harrell-Cook, G., & Dulebohn, J. H. (2000). *Organizational politics: The nature of the relationship between politics perceptions and political behavior. In Research in the Sociology of Organizations*. Emerald Group Publishing Limited, Bingley, UK, 89-130.

Ferris, G. R., Russ, G. S., & Fandt, P. M. (1989). Politics in Organizations. In *Impression Management in the Organization*, eds. RA Giacalone and P. Rosenfield, 143-170. Erlbaum, Hillsdale, NJ.

Ferris, G. R., Berkson, H. M., Kaplan, D. M., Gilmore, D. C., Buckley, M. R., Hochwarter, W. A., & Witt, L. A. (1999). Development and initial validation of the political skill inventory. In *Academy of Management, 59th Annual National Meeting*, Chicago (pp. 6-11).

Ferris, G. R., Treadway, D. C., Brouer, R. L., & Munyon, T. P. (2012). Political skill in the organizational sciences. *Politics in Organizations: Theory and Research Considerations*. New York.

Ferris, G. R., Adams, G., Kolodinsky, R. W., Hochwarter, W. A., & Ammeter, A. P. (2002). Perceptions of organizational politics: Theory and research directions. *Research in Multi-Level Issues, The Many Faces of Multi-Level Issues*. JAI Press/Elsevier, Oxford.

Folger, R., Konovsky, M. A., & Cropanzano, R. (1992). A due process metaphor for performance appraisal. *Research in organizational behavior*, 14, 129-129.

Franke, H., & Foerstl, K. (2018). Fostering integrated research on organizational politics and conflict in teams: A cross-phenomenal review. *European Management Journal*, 36(5), 593-607.

Freeman, D., McManus, S., Brugha, T., Meltzer, H., Jenkins, R., & Bebbington, P. (2011). Concomitants of paranoia in the general population. *Psychological Medicine*, 41(5), 923-36.

French, J., Rodgers, W. and Cobb, S. (1974). *Adjustment as person-environment fit. Coping and adaptation.* Basic Books, New York.

Fudge, R.S., & Schlacter, J. L. (1999). Motivating employees to act ethically: An expectancy theory approach. *Journal of Business Ethics*, 18(3), 295-304.

Gallagher, V. C., & Laird, M. D. (2008). The Combined Effect of Political Skill and Political Decision Making on Job Satisfaction. *Journal of Applied Social Psychology*, 38(9), 2336-2360.

Gandz, J., & Murray, V. V. (1980). The experience of workplace politics. *Academy of Management Journal*, 23(2), 237-251.

García-Chas, R., Neira-Fontela, E., Varela-Neira, C., & Curto-Rodríguez, E. (2019). The effect of political skill on work role performance and intention to leave: A moderated mediation model. *Journal of Leadership & Organizational Studies*, 26(1), 98-110.

Gelfand, M.J., Raver, J.L., Nishii, L., Leslie, L.M., Lun, J., Lim, B.C., Duan, L., Almaliach, A., Ang, S., Arnadottir, J., & Aycan, Z. (2011). Differences between tight and loose cultures: A 33-nation study. *Science*, 332(6033), 1100-1104.

Glick, N. L. (1992). Job satisfaction among academic administrators. *Research in Higher Education*, 33(5), 625-639.

Glick, P., & Fiske, S. T. (1996). The ambivalent sexism inventory: Differentiating hostile and benevolent sexism. *Journal of Personality and Social Psychology* 70, 491-512.

Grant, A. M., Fried, Y., Parker, S. K., & Frese, M. (2010). Putting job design in context: Introduction to the special issue. *The Journal of Organizational Behaviour*, 31, 145-157.

Grant, A. M., Fried, Y., Parker, S. K., & Frese, M. (2010). Putting job design in context: Introduction to the special issue. *Journal of Organizational Behavior*, 31(2-3), 145-57.

Greenbaum, R. L., Hill, A., Mawritz, M. B., & Quade, M. J. (2017). Employee Machiavellianism to unethical behavior: The role of abusive supervision as a trait activator. *Journal of Management*, 43(2), 585-609.

Hackman, J.R., & Oldham, G. R. (1980). *Work Redesign.* Addison Wesley, Reading, MA.

Haggard, D. L., Robert, C., & Rose, A. J. (2011). Co-rumination in the workplace: Adjustment trade-offs for men and women who engage in excessive discussions of workplace problems. *Journal of Business and Psychology, 26*(1), 27-40.

Haider, S., Fatima, N., & de Pablos-Heredero, C. (2020). A three-wave longitudinal study of moderated mediation between perceptions of politics and employee turnover intentions: the role of job anxiety and political skills. *Journal of Work and Organizational Psychology*, 36(1), 1-14.

Hair, J. F., Black, W., Babin, B., Anderson, R., & Tathum, R. (2006). *Multivariate Data Analysis.* Upper Saddle River: Prentice Hall.

Han, G. H., Harms, P. D., & Bai, Y. (2017). Nightmare bosses: The impact of abusive supervision on employees' sleep, emotions, and creativity. *Journal of Business Ethics, 145*(1), 21-31.

Harris, K. J., Kacmar, K. M., Zivnuska, S., & Shaw, J. D. (2007). The impact of political skill on impression management effectiveness. *Journal of Applied Psychology*, 92(1), 278-285.

Harris, K. J., Harvey, P., Harris, R. B., & Cast, M. (2013). An investigation of abusive supervision, vicarious abusive supervision, and their joint impacts. *The Journal of Social Psychology*, 153(1), 38-50.

Harris, K. J., Harris, R. B., & Brouer, R. L. (2009). LMX and subordinate political skill: Direct and interactive effects on turnover intentions and job satisfaction. *Journal of Applied Social Psychology*, 39(10), 2373-2395.

Harris, L. C., & Ogbonna, E. (2006). Service sabotage: A study of antecedents and consequences. *Journal of the Academy of Marketing Science*, 34(4), 543-558.

Harrison, D. A., McLaughlin, M. E., & Coalter, T. M. (1996). Context, cognition, and common method variance: Psychometric and verbal protocol evidence. *Organizational Behavior and Human Decision Processes*, 68(3), 246-261.

Harvey, P., Stoner, J., Hochwarter, W., & Kacmar, C. (2007). Coping with abusive supervision: The neutralizing effects of ingratiation and positive affect on negative employee outcomes. *The Leadership Quarterly*, 18(3), 264-280.

Harvey, P., Harris, R. B., Harris, K. J., & Wheeler, A. R. (2007). Attenuating the effects of social stress: The impact of political skill. Journal of Occupational Health Psychology, 12(2), 105-15.

Hayes, A. F. (2013). *An introduction to mediation, moderation, and conditional process analysis*, The Guilford Press, New York.

Heale, R., & Twycross, A. (2015). Validity and reliability in quantitative studies. *Evidence-Based Nursing*, 18(3), 66-7.

Heider, F. (1958). *The Psychology of Interpersonal Relations*, Wiley, New York, NY.

Herzberg, F., Mausner, B., & Snyderman, B. B. (1959). *The Motivation to Work.* John Wiley & Sons, New York.

Hobfoll, S. E. (1989). Conservation of resources: A new attempt at conceptualizing stress. *American Psychologist*, 44(3), 513-524.

Hobfoll, S. E. (2001). The influence of culture, community, and the nested-self in the stress process: Advancing conservation of resources theory. *Applied Psychology*, 50(3), 337-421.

Hochwarter, W. A., Witt, L. A., Treadway, D. C., & Ferris, G. R. (2006). The interaction of social skill and organizational support on job performance. *Journal of Applied Psychology*, 91(2), 482-489.

Hochwarter, W. A., Kiewitz, C., Castro, S. L., Perrewè, P. L., & Ferris, G. R. (2003). Positive affectivity and collective efficacy as moderators of the relationship between perceived politics and job satisfaction. *Journal of Applied Social Psychology*, 33(5), 1009-1035.

Hu, L. T., & Bentler, P. M. (1999). Cutoff criteria for fit indexes in covariance structure analysis: Conventional criteria versus new alternatives. *Structural Equation Modeling: A Multidisciplinary Journal*, 6(1), 1-55.

Hutchinson, D. M. (2015). *Employee retaliation against abusive supervision: testing the distinction between overt and covert retaliation*. Master Dissertation. University of South Florida.

Ilies, R., & Judge, T. A. (2004). An experience-sampling measure of job satisfaction and its relationships with affectivity, mood at work, job beliefs, and general job satisfaction. *European Journal of Work and Organizational Psychology*, 13(3), 367-389.

Inegbedion, H., Inegbedion, E., Peter, A., & Harry, L. (2020). Perception of workload balance and employee job satisfaction in work organisations. *Heliyon*, 6(1), e03160.

Jakobsen, M., & Jensen, R. (2015). Common method bias in public management studies. *International Public Management Journal*, 18(1), 3-30.

Jawahar, I. M., Stone, T. H., & Kisamore, J. L. (2007). Role conflict and burnout: The direct and moderating effects of political skill and perceived organizational support on burnout dimensions. *International Journal of Stress Management*, 14(2), 142-59.

Jezl, D. R., Molidor, C. E., & Wright, T. L. (1996). Physical, sexual and psychological abuse in high school dating relationships: Prevalence rates and self-esteem issues. *Child and Adolescent Social Work Journal*, 13(1), 69-87.

Jiang, Z., Di Milia, L., Jiang, Y., & Jiang, X. (2020). Thriving at work: A mentoring-moderated process linking task identity and autonomy to job satisfaction. *Journal of Vocational Behavior*, 118, 103373.

Jóhannsdóttir, H. L., & Ólafsson, R. F. (2004). Coping with bullying in the workplace: The effect of gender, age and type of bullying. *British Journal of Guidance & Counselling*, 32(3), 319-333.

Johnson, R. E., Venus, M., Lanaj, K., Mao, C., & Chang, C. H. (2012). Leader identity as an antecedent of the frequency and consistency of transformational, consideration, and abusive leadership behaviors. *Journal of Applied Psychology*, 97(6), 1262-72.

Jonason, P. K., Slomski, S., & Partyka, J. (2012). The Dark Triad at work: How toxic employees get their way. *Personality and individual differences*, 52(3), 449-453.

Jones, E. E. (1990). *Interpersonal perception,* Freeman, New York.

Joo, B. K. B., & Park, S. (2010). Career satisfaction, organizational commitment, and turnover intention: The effects of goal orientation, organizational learning culture and developmental feedback. *Leadership & Organization Development Journal*, 31(6), 482-500.

Ju, D., Huang, M., Liu, D., Qin, X., Hu, Q., & Chen, C. (2019). Supervisory consequences of abusive supervision: An investigation of sense of power, managerial self-efficacy, and task-oriented leadership behavior. *Organizational Behavior and Human Decision Processes*, 154, 80-95.

Judge, T. A., Bono, J. E., Ilies, R., & Gerhardt, M. W. (2002). Personality and leadership: a qualitative and quantitative review. *Journal of Applied Psychology*, 87(4), 765-780.

Jyoti, J., & Rani, A. (2019). Role of burnout and mentoring between high performance work system and intention to leave: Moderated mediation model. *Journal of Business Research*, 98, 166-176.

Kacmar, K.M., & Carlson, D.S. (1997). Further validation of the perceptions of politics scale (POPS): A multiple sample investigation." *Journal of Management*, 23(5), 627-58.

Kacmar, K. M., & Ferris, G. R. (1991). Perceptions of organizational politics scale (POPS): Development and construct validation. *Educational and Psychological Measurement*, 51(1), 193-205.

Kacmar, K. M., Andrews, M. C., Harris, K. J., & Tepper, B. J. (2013). Ethical leadership and subordinate outcomes: The mediating role of organizational politics and the moderating role of political skill. *Journal of Business Ethics*, 115(1), 33-44.

Kaplan, D.M. (2008). Political choices: The role of political skill in occupational choice. *Career Development International*, 13, 46-55.

Kapoutsis, I., Papalexandris, A., Nikolopoulos, A., Hochwarter, W. A., & Ferris, G. R. (2011). Politics perceptions as moderator of the political skill–job performance relationship: A two-study, cross-national, constructive replication. *Journal of vocational Behavior*, 78(1), 123-135.

Karatepe, O. M., Kim, T. T., & Lee, G. (2019). Is political skill really an antidote in the workplace incivility-emotional exhaustion and outcome relationship in the hotel industry? *Journal of Hospitality and Tourism Management*, 40, 40-49.

Kelemen, M. and Rumens, N. (2008). *An Introduction to Critical Management Research.* Sage, London.

Schat, A. C., Frone, M. R., & Kelloway, E. K. (2006). Prevalence of Workplace Aggression in the US Workforce: Findings From a National Study. *Handbook of workplace violence.* Sage, Thousand Oaks, CA.

Kernan, M. C., Watson, S., Chen, F. F., & Kim, T. G. (2011). How cultural values affect the impact of abusive supervision on worker attitudes. *Cross Cultural Management: An International Journal*, 18(4), 464-484.

Khan, A. K., Moss, S., Quratulain, S., & Hameed, I. (2018). When and how subordinate performance leads to abusive supervision: A social dominance perspective. *Journal of Management*, 44(7), 2801-2826.

Khan, A. K., Quratulain, S., & Crawshaw, J. R. (2017). Double jeopardy: Subordinates' worldviews and poor performance as predictors of abusive supervision. *Journal of Business and Psychology*, 32(2), 165-178.

Zhiqiang, M., Abubakari Sadick, M., & Ibn Musah, A. A. (2018). Investigating the role of psychological contract breach, political skill and work ethic on perceived politics and job attitudes relationships: A case of higher education in Pakistan. *Sustainability*, 10(12), 4737.

Kiazad, K., Restubog, S. L. D., Zagenczyk, T. J., Kiewitz, C., & Tang, R. L. (2010). In pursuit of power: The role of authoritarian leadership in the relationship between supervisors' Machiavellianism and subordinates' perceptions of abusive supervisory behavior. *Journal of Research in Personality*, 44(4), 512-519.

Kiewitz, C., Restubog, S. L. D., Zagenczyk, T. J., Scott, K. D., Garcia, P. R. J. M., & Tang, R. L. (2012). Sins of the parents: Self-control as a buffer between supervisors' previous experience of family undermining and subordinates' perceptions of abusive supervision. *The Leadership Quarterly*, 23(5), 869-882.

Kim, S. (2005). Factors affecting state government information technology employee turnover intentions. *The American Review of Public Administration*, 35(2), 137-156.

Kimberlin, C. L., & Winterstein, A. G. (2008). Validity and reliability of measurement instruments used in research. *American Journal of Health-System Pharmacy*, 65(23), 2276-2284.

Kimura, T. (2015). A review of political skill: Current research trend and directions for future research. *International Journal of Management Reviews*, 17(3), 312-332.

Kimura, T., Bande, B., & Fernández-Ferrín, P. (2019). The roles of political skill and intrinsic motivation in performance prediction of adaptive selling. *Industrial Marketing Management*, 77, 198-208.

Knippen, J. M., Shen, W., & Zhu, Q. (2019). Limited progress? The effect of external pressure for board gender diversity on the increase of female directors. *Strategic Management Journal*, 40(7), 1123-1150.

Kolodinsky, R. W., Hochwarter, W. A., & Ferris, G. R. (2004). Nonlinearity in the relationship between political skill and work outcomes: Convergent evidence from three studies. *Journal of Vocational Behavior*, 65(2), 294-308.

Korsakienė, R., Stankevičienė, A., Šimelytė, A., & Talačkienė, M. (2015). Factors driving turnover and retention of information technology professionals. *Journal of Business Economics and Management*, 16(1), 1-17.

Kowal, J., & Roztocki, N. (2015). Job satisfaction of IT professionals in Poland: does business competence matter? *Journal of Business Economics and Management*, 16(5), 995-1012.

La, I. S., & Yun, E. K. (2019). Effects of trait anger and anger expression on job satisfaction and burnout in preceptor nurses and newly graduated nurses: A dyadic analysis. *Asian Nursing Research*, 13(4), 242-248.

Labrague, L. J., McEnroe-Petitte, D. M., Gloe, D., Tsaras, K., Arteche, D. L., & Maldia, F. (2017). Organizational politics, nurses' stress, burnout levels, turnover intention and job satisfaction. *International Nursing Review*, 64(1), 109-116.

Laird, M. D., Zboja, J. J., & Ferris, G. R. (2012). Partial mediation of the political skill-reputation relationship. *Career Development International*, 17(6), 557-82.

Lau, C. M., Scully, G., & Lee, A. (2018). The effects of organizational politics on employee motivations to participate in target setting and employee budgetary participation. *Journal of Business Research*, 90, 247-259.

Lawler, J. J., Walumbwa, F. O., & Bai, B. (2007). National culture and cultural effects. In *Handbook of Research in International Human Resource Management*, Lawrence-Erlbaum, New York, NY.

Lee, F., Hallahan, M., & Herzog, T. (1996). Explaining real-life events: How culture and domain shape attributions. *Personality and Social Psychology Bulletin*, 22(7), 732-741.

Lee, T. W., Mitchell, T. R., Holtom, B. C., McDaneil, L. S., & Hill, J. W. (1999). The unfolding model of voluntary turnover: A replication and extension. *Academy of Management Journal*, 42(4), 450-462.

Lee, T. W., & Mowday, R. T. (1987). Voluntarily leaving an organization: An empirical investigation of Steers and Mowday's model of turnover. *Academy of Management Journal*, 30(4), 721-743.

Leung, A. S., Wu, L. Z., Chen, Y. Y., & Young, M. N. (2011). The impact of workplace ostracism in service organizations. *International Journal of Hospitality Management*, 30(4), 836-844.

Lewin, K. (1936). *Principles of topological psychology*. McGraw-Hill, New York.

Li, J., Sun, G., & Cheng, Z. (2017). The influence of political skill on salespersons' work outcomes: A resource perspective. *Journal of Business Ethics*, 141(3), 551-562.

Li, X., Qian, J., Han, Z. R., & Jin, Z. (2016). Coping with abusive supervision: the neutralizing effects of perceived organizational support and political skill on employees' burnout. *Current Psychology*, 35(1), 77-82.

Lian, H., Ferris, D. L., & Brown, D. J. (2012). Does taking the good with the bad make things worse? How abusive supervision and leader–member exchange interact to impact need satisfaction and organizational deviance. *Organizational Behavior and Human Decision Processes*, 117(1), 41-52.

Liang, L. H., Lian, H., Brown, D. J., Ferris, D. L., Hanig, S., & Keeping, L. M. (2016). Why are abusive supervisors abusive? A dual-system self-control model. *Academy of Management Journal*, 59(4), 1385-1406.

Liden, R. C., Wayne, S. J., & Stilwell, D. (1993). A longitudinal study on the early development of leader-member exchanges. Journal of applied psychology, 78(4), 662-674.

Iimura, S., & Taku, K. (2018). Gender differences in relationship between resilience and big five personality traits in Japanese adolescents. *Psychological Reports*, 121(5), 920-931.

Ling, F. Y. Y., & Loo, C. M. (2015). Characteristics of jobs and jobholders that affect job satisfaction and work performance of project managers. *Journal of Management in Engineering*, 31(3), 04014039.

Liu, D., Liao, H., & Loi, R. (2012). The dark side of leadership: A three-level investigation of the cascading effect of abusive supervision on employee creativity. *Academy of Management Journal*, 55(5), 1187-1212.

Liu, H. Y., Chao, C. Y., Kain, V. J., & Sung, S. C. (2019). The relationship of personal competencies, social adaptation, and job adaptation on job satisfaction. *Nurse Education Today*, 83, 104199.

Liu, Y., & Liu, X. Y. (2018). Politics under abusive supervision: The role of Machiavellianism and guanxi. *European Management Journal*, 36(5), 649-659.

Liu, Y., Ferris, G. R., Treadway, D. C., Prati, M. L., Perrewé, P. L., & Hochwarter, W. A. (2006). The emotion of politics and the politics of emotions: Affective and cognitive reactions to politics as a stressor. *Handbook of Organizational Politics*, Edward Elgar, Northampton, MA.

Liu, Y., Ferris, G. R., Zinko, R., Perrewé, P. L., Weitz, B., & Xu, J. (2007). Dispositional antecedents and outcomes of political skill in organizations: A four-study investigation with convergence. *Journal of Vocational Behavior*, 71(1), 146-165.

Locke, E. A. (1969). What is job satisfaction? *Organizational Behavior and Human Performance*, 4(4), 309-336.

Locke, E. A. (1970). Job satisfaction and job performance: A theoretical analysis. Organizational behavior and human performance, 5(5), 484-500.

Locke, E. A., & Henne, D. (1986). Work motivation theories. *International review of Industrial and Organizational Psychology*, 1, 1-35.

Lu, H., Zhao, Y., & While, A. (2019). Job satisfaction among hospital nurses: A literature review. *International Journal of Nursing Studies*, 94, 21-31.

Luthans, F., Hodgetts, R. M., & Rosenkrantz, S. A. (1988). *Real Managers* (Ballinger, Cambridge, MA).

Lynn, R., & Martin, T. (1997). Gender differences in extraversion, neuroticism, and psychoticism in 37 nations. *The Journal of Social Psychology*, 137(3), 369-373.

Lyu, D., Ji, L., Zheng, Q., Yu, B., & Fan, Y. (2019). Abusive supervision and turnover intention: Mediating effects of psychological empowerment of nurses. *International Journal of Nursing Sciences*, 6(2), 198-203.

Mackey, J. D., Frieder, R. E., Brees, J. R., & Martinko, M. J. (2017). Abusive supervision: A meta-analysis and empirical review. *Journal of Management*, 43(6), 1940-1965.

Mahajan, A., & Toh, S. M. (2017). Group cultural values and political skills: A situationist perspective on interpersonal citizenship behaviors. *Journal of International Business Studies*, 48(1), 113-121.

Mahdi, A. F., Zin, M. Z. M., Nor, M. R. M., Sakat, A. A., & Naim, A. S. A. (2012). The relationship between job satisfaction and turnover intention. *American Journal of Applied Sciences*, 9(9), 1518-1526.

Maher, L. P., Gallagher, V. C., Rossi, A. M., Ferris, G. R., & Perrewé, P. L. (2018). Political skill and will as predictors of impression management frequency and style: A three-study investigation. *Journal of Vocational Behavior*, 107, 276-294.

Malik, O. F., Shahzad, A., Raziq, M. M., Khan, M. M., Yusaf, S., & Khan, A. (2019). Perceptions of organizational politics, knowledge hiding, and employee creativity: The moderating role of professional commitment. *Personality and Individual Differences*, 142, 232-237.

March, J. G. and Simon, H. A. (1958). *Organizations*, John Wiley, New York, NY.

Marsh, H. W., Hau, K. T., & Wen, Z. (2004). In search of golden rules: Comment on hypothesis-testing approaches to setting cutoff values for fit indexes and dangers in overgeneralizing Hu and Bentler's (1999) findings. *Structural equation modeling*, 11(3), 320-341.

Martinko, M. J., Harvey, P., Brees, J. R., & Mackey, J. (2013). A review of abusive supervision research. *Journal of Organizational Behavior*, 34(1), 120-137.

Mawritz, M. B., Mayer, D. M., Hoobler, J. M., Wayne, S. J., & Marinova, S. V. (2012). A trickle-down model of abusive supervision. *Personnel Psychology*, 65(2), 325-357.

Mawritz, M. B., Greenbaum, R. L., Butts, M. M., & Graham, K. A. (2017). I just can't control myself: A self-regulation perspective on the abuse of deviant employees. *Academy of Management Journal*, 60(4), 1482-1503.

McAllister, C. P., Ellen III, B. P., & Ferris, G. R. (2018). Social influence opportunity recognition, evaluation, and capitalization: Increased theoretical specification through political skill's dimensional dynamics. *Journal of Management*, 44(5), 1926-1952.

Madison, D. L., Allen, R. W., Porter, L. W., Renwick, P. A., & Mayes, B. T. (1980). Organizational politics: An exploration of managers' perceptions. *Human relations*, 33(2), 79-100.

Meisler, G. (2014). Exploring emotional intelligence, political skill, and job satisfaction. *Employee Relations*, 36, 280-93.

Meisler, G., & Vigoda-Gadot, E. (2014). Perceived organizational politics, emotional intelligence and work outcomes: Empirical exploration of direct and indirect effects, *Personnel Review*, 43(1), 116-135.

Meurs, J. A., Gallagher, V. C., & Perrewé, P. L. (2010). The role of political skill in the stressor–outcome relationship: Differential predictions for self-and other-reports of political skill. *Journal of Vocational Behavior*, 76(3), 520-533.

Meyer, J. P., & Allen, N. J. (1997). *Commitment in the Workplace: Theory, Research, and Application.* Sage, Thousand Oaks, CA.

Michaels, C. E., & Spector, P. E. (1982). Causes of employee turnover: A test of the Mobley, Griffeth, Hand, and Meglino model. *Journal of Applied Psychology*, 67(1), 53-59.

Miller, B. K., Rutherford, M. A., & Kolodinsky, R. W. (2008). Perceptions of organizational politics: A meta-analysis of outcomes. *Journal of Business and Psychology*, 22(3), 209-222.

Mintzberg, H. (1983). *Power in and around organizations.* Prentice-Hall, Englewood Cliffs, NJ.

Mintzberg, H. (1985). The organization as political arena. *Journal of Management Studies*, 22(2), 133-154.

Mischel, W. (1968). *Personality and assessment*, Wiley, New York, NY.

Mitchell, M. S., & Ambrose, M. L. (2007). Abusive supervision and workplace deviance and the moderating effects of negative reciprocity beliefs. Journal of applied psychology, 92(4), 1159-1168.

Mitchell, T. R. (1974). Expectancy models of job satisfaction, occupational preference and effort: A theoretical, methodological, and empirical appraisal. Psychological Bulletin, 81(12), 1053-1077.

Mobley, W. H., Horner, S. O., & Hollingsworth, A. T. (1978). An evaluation of precursors of hospital employee turnover. *Journal of Applied Psychology*, 63(4), 408-14.

Molm, L. D. (1997). *Coercive power in social exchange.* Cambridge Univ. Press, Cambridge.

Mottaz, C. J. (1988). Determinants of organizational commitment. *Human Relations*, 41(6), 467-482.

Moynihan, D. P., & Landuyt, N. (2008). Explaining turnover intention in state government: Examining the roles of gender, life cycle, and loyalty. *Review of Public Personnel Administration*, 28(2), 120-143.

Munyon, T. P., Summers, J. K., Thompson, K. M., & Ferris, G. R. (2015). Political skill and work outcomes: A theoretical extension, meta-analytic investigation, and agenda for the future. *Personnel Psychology*, 68(1), 143-184.

Naseer, S., Raja, U., Syed, F., Donia, M. B., & Darr, W. (2016). Perils of being close to a bad leader in a bad environment: Exploring the combined effects of despotic leadership, leader member exchange, and perceived organizational politics on behaviors. *The Leadership Quarterly*, 27(1), 14-33.

Ng, S. B. C., Chen, Z. X., & Aryee, S. (2012). Abusive supervision in Chinese work settings. In *Handbook of Chinese Organizational Behavior: Integrating theory, research and practice*, Edward Elgar Publishing Limited, Cheltenham, UK.

Nickerson, R. S. (1998). Confirmation bias: A ubiquitous phenomenon in many guises. *Review of General Psychology*, 2(2), 175-220.

Ouyang, K., Lam, W., & Wang, W. (2015). Roles of gender and identification on abusive supervision and proactive behavior. *Asia Pacific Journal of Management*, 32(3), 671-691.

Pakistan Bureau of Statistics (2018). Labour Force Participation Rates and Un-Employment Rates by Age, Sex and Area 2017-18. In *Labour Force Survey 2017-18*, Thirty-fourth issue, Government of Pakistan Ministry of Statistics Pakistan Bureau of Statistics, Islamabad, Pakistan. https://www.pbs.gov.pk/sites/default/files//Labour%20Force/publications/lfs2017_18/Annual%20Report%20of%20LFS%202017-18.pdf

Park, J. (2016). The moderating effects of leader-member exchange and proactive voice behavior on the relationships between perceptions of organizational politics and employee attitudes. *Korean Journal of Organization and Management*, 40(3), 31-58.

Park, J. C., Kim, S., & Lee, H. (2020). Effect of work-related smartphone use after work on job burnout: Moderating effect of social support and organizational politics. *Computers in Human Behavior*, 105, 106194.

Park, J., & Kim, H. J. (2019). How and when does abusive supervision affect hospitality employees' service sabotage? *International Journal of Hospitality Management*, 83, 190-197.

Paulhus, D. L., & Williams, K. M. (2002). The dark triad of personality: Narcissism, Machiavellianism, and psychopathy. *Journal of Research in Personality*, 36(6), 556-563.

Perrewé, P. L., Zellars, K. L., Ferris, G. R., Rossi, A. M., Kacmar, C. J., & Ralston, D. A. (2004). Neutralizing job stressors: Political skill as an antidote to the dysfunctional consequences of role conflict. *Academy of Management Journal*, 47(1), 141-152.

Perrewé, P. L., Zellars, K. L., Rossi, A. M., Ferris, G. R., Kacmar, C. J., Liu, Y., ... & Hochwarter, W. A. (2005). Political Skill: An Antidote in the Role Overload–Strain Relationship. *Journal of Occupational Health Psychology*, 10(3), 239-50.

Pfeffer, J. (1981). Management as symbolic action: the creation and maintenance of organizational paradigm. *Research in Organizational Behavior*, 3, 1-52.

Pfeffer, J. (1981). *Power in organizations*, Pitman, Marshfield, MA.

Pfeffer, J. (1992). *Managing with power*. Harvard University Press, Boston, MA.

Plouffe, C. R., & Barclay, D. W. (2007). Salesperson navigation: The intraorganizational dimension of the sales role. *Industrial Marketing Management*, 36(4), 528-539.

Podsakoff, P. M., MacKenzie, S. B., & Podsakoff, N. P. (2012). Sources of method bias in social science research and recommendations on how to control it. *Annual Review of Psychology*, 63, 539-569.

Podsakoff, P. M., MacKenzie, S. B., Lee, J. Y., & Podsakoff, N. P. (2003). Common method biases in behavioral research: a critical review of the literature and recommended remedies. *Journal of Applied Psychology*, 88(5), 879-903.

Qian, J., & Li, X. (2016). Supervisory mentoring and employee feedback seeking: the moderating effects of power distance and political skill. *Current Psychology*, 35(3), 486-494.

Reio Jr, T. G. (2010). The threat of common method variance bias to theory building. *Human Resource Development Review*, 9(4), 405-411.

Restubog, S. L. D., Scott, K. L., & Zagenczyk, T. J. (2011). When distress hits home: The role of contextual factors and psychological distress in predicting employees' responses to abusive supervision. *Journal of Applied Psychology*, 96(4), 713-29

Rhoades, L., & Eisenberger, R. (2002). Perceived organizational support: a review of the literature. *Journal of Applied Psychology*, 87(4), 698-714.

Richardson, H. A., Simmering, M. J., & Sturman, M. C. (2009). A tale of three perspectives: Examining post hoc statistical techniques for detection and correction of common method variance. *Organizational Research Methods*, 12(4), 762-800.

Richardson, H. A., Simmering, M. J., & Sturman, M. C. (2009). A tale of three perspectives: Examining post hoc statistical techniques for detection and correction of common method variance. *Organizational Research Methods*, 12(4), 762-800.

Richer, S. F., Blanchard, C., & Vallerand, R. J. (2002). A motivational model of work turnover. *Journal of Applied Social Psychology*, 32(10), 2089-2113.

Robbins, S. P. (2003). *Organizational Behavior*. Prentice Hall, New Jersey.

Roberts, J. A., & David, M. E. (2020). Boss phubbing, trust, job satisfaction and employee performance. *Personality and Individual Differences*, 155, 109702.

Rosen, C. C., Harris, K. J., & Kacmar, K. M. (2009). The emotional implications of organizational politics: A process model. *Human relations*, 62(1), 27-57.

Rubenstein, A. L., Eberly, M. B., Lee, T. W., & Mitchell, T. R. (2018). Surveying the forest: A meta-analysis, moderator investigation, and future-oriented discussion of the antecedents of voluntary employee turnover. *Personnel Psychology*, 71(1), 23-65.

Saunders, M. N., Lewis, P., Thornhill, A., & Bristow, A. (2015). Understanding research philosophy and approaches to theory development. Chapter 4, (122-161) In *Research Methods for Business Students*, 7th Edition, Pearson.

Schermelleh-Engel, K., Moosbrugger, H., & Müller, H. (2003). Evaluating the fit of structural equation models: Tests of significance and descriptive goodness-of-fit measures. *Methods of Psychological Research Online*, 8(2), 23-74.

Shan, Y., Imran, H., Lewis, P., & Zhai, D. (2017). Investigating the latent factors of quality of work-life affecting construction craft worker job satisfaction. *Journal of Construction Engineering and Management*, 143(5), 04016134.

Sharpe, D. R. (2006). Shop floor practices under changing forms of managerial control: A comparative ethnographic study of micro-politics, control and resistance within a Japanese multinational. *Journal of International Management*, 12(3), 318-339.

Shepard, M. F., & Campbell, J. A. (1992). The Abusive Behavior Inventory: A measure of psychological and physical abuse. *Journal of Interpersonal Violence*, 7(3), 291-305.

Shi, J., Chen, Z., & Zhou, L. (2011). Testing differential mediation effects of sub-dimensions of political skills in linking proactive personality to employee performance. *Journal of Business and Psychology*, 26(3), 359-369.

Smith, M. B., & Webster, B. D. (2017). A moderated mediation model of Machiavellianism, social undermining, political skill, and supervisor-rated job performance. *Personality and Individual Differences*, 104, 453-459.

Smith, P. K., Shu, S., & Madsen, K. (2001). Characteristics of victims of school bullying. *Peer harassment in school: The plight of the vulnerable and victimized*, 332-351.

Stengel, R. (2000.) *You're too kind: A brief history of flattery.* Simon & Schuster, New York, NY.

Suhr, D. D. (2006). *Exploratory or confirmatory factor analysis?* Statistics and Data Analysis.

Summers, J. K., Munyon, T. P., Brouer, R. L., Pahng, P., & Ferris, G. R. (2020). Political skill in the stressor-strain relationship: A meta-analytic update and extension. *Journal of Vocational Behavior*, 118, 103372.

Swann, W. B. (2012). Self-verification theory. *Handbook of Theories of Social Psychology.* Sage, London.

Syed, J., & Ali, F. (2019). Theorizing equal opportunity in Muslim majority countries. *Gender, Work & Organization*, 26(11), 1621-1639.

Syed, J., & Tariq, M. (2017). Paradox of gender and leadership in India: A critical review of Mardaani. *South Asian Journal of Business Studies*, 6(3), 365-79.

Taliadorou, N., & Pashiardis, P. (2015). Examining the role of emotional intelligence and political skill to educational leadership and their effects to teachers' job satisfaction. *Journal of Educational Administration*, 53(5), 642-666.

Tedeschi, J. T., & Felson, R. B. (1994). *Violence, Aggression, and Coercive Actions.* Am. Psychological Association, Washington, DC.

Tedeschi, J. T., & Norman, N. M. (1985). A social psychological interpretation of displaced aggression. *Adv. Group Process,* 2, 29-56.

Tehseen, S., Ramayah, T., & Sajilan, S. (2017). Testing and controlling for common method variance: A review of available methods. *Journal of Management Sciences*, 4(2), 142-168.

Templer, K. J. (2018). Dark personality, job performance ratings, and the role of political skill: An indication of why toxic people may get ahead at work. *Personality and Individual Differences*, 124, 209-214.

Tepper, B. J. (2000). Consequences of abusive supervision. *Academy of Management Journal*, 43(2), 178-190.

Tepper, B. J. (2007). Abusive supervision in work organizations: Review, synthesis, and research agenda. *Journal of Management*, 33(3), 261-289.

Tepper, B. J., Simon, L., & Park, H. M. (2017). Abusive supervision. *Annual Review of Organizational Psychology and Organizational Behavior*, 4, 123-52.

Tepper, B. J., Duffy, M. K., Henle, C. A., & Lambert, L. S. (2006). Procedural injustice, victim precipitation, and abusive supervision. *Personnel Psychology*, 59(1), 101-123.

Tepper, B. J., Moss, S. E., & Duffy, M. K. (2011). Predictors of abusive supervision: Supervisor perceptions of deep-level dissimilarity, relationship conflict, and subordinate performance. *Academy of Management Journal*, 54(2), 279-294.

Tett, R. P., & Meyer, J. P. (1993). Job satisfaction, organizational commitment, turnover intention, and turnover: path analyses based on meta-analytic findings. *Personnel Psychology*, 46(2), 259-293.

Thau, S., Bennett, R. J., Mitchell, M. S., & Marrs, M. B. (2009). How management style moderates the relationship between abusive supervision and workplace deviance: An uncertainty management theory perspective. *Organizational Behavior and Human Decision Processes*, 108(1), 79-92.

Toh, S. M., & Leonardelli, G. J. (2012). Cultural constraints on the emergence of women as leaders. *Journal of World Business*, 47(4), 604-611.

Ton, Z., & Huckman, R. S. (2008). Managing the impact of employee turnover on performance: The role of process conformance. *Organization Science*, 19(1), 56-68.

Treadway, D. C., Ferris, G. R., Duke, A. B., Adams, G. L., & Thatcher, J. B. (2007). The moderating role of subordinate political skill on supervisors' impressions of subordinate ingratiation and ratings of subordinate interpersonal facilitation. *Journal of Applied Psychology*, 92(3), 848-55.

Treadway, D. C., Ferris, G. R., Hochwarter, W., Perrewé, P., Witt, L. A., & Goodman, J. M. (2005). The role of age in the perceptions of politics--job performance relationship: a three-study constructive replication. *Journal of Applied Psychology*, 90(5), 872-81.

Treadway, D. C., Hochwarter, W. A., Ferris, G. R., Kacmar, C. J., Douglas, C., Ammeter, A. P., & Buckley, M. R. (2004). Leader political skill and employee reactions. *The Leadership Quarterly*, 15(4), 493-513.

Treadway, D. C., Hochwarter, W. A., Kacmar, C. J., & Ferris, G. R. (2005). Political will, political skill, and political behavior. *Journal of Organizational Behavior: The International Journal of Industrial, Occupational and Organizational Psychology and Behavior*, 26(3), 229-245.

Triandis, H. C. (1989). The self and social behavior in differing cultural contexts. *Psychological Review*, 96(3), 506-520.

Triplett, N. (1898). The dynamogenic factors in pacemaking and competition. *The American Journal of Psychology*, 9(4), 507-533.

Ünal, A. F., Warren, D. E., & Chen, C. C. (2012). The normative foundations of unethical supervision in organizations. *Journal of Business Ethics*, 107(1), 5-19.

Valle, M., & Perrewe, P. L. (2000). Do politics perceptions relate to political behaviors? Tests of an implicit assumption and expanded model. *Human Relations*, 53(3), 359-386.

Van Eerde, W., & Thierry, H. (1996). Vroom's expectancy models and work-related criteria: A meta-analysis. Journal of applied psychology, 81(5), 575-586.

Vigoda, E. (2000). Organizational politics, job attitudes, and work outcomes: Exploration and implications for the public sector. *Journal of Vocational Behavior*, 57(3), 326-347.

Vigoda, E., & Cohen, A. (2002). Influence tactics and perceptions of organizational politics: A longitudinal study. *Journal of Business Research*, 55(4), 311-324.

Visher, C. A. (1983). Gender, police arrest decisions, and notions of chivalry. *Criminology*, 21(1), 5-28.

Vogel, R. M., Mitchell, M. S., Tepper, B. J., Restubog, S. L., Hu, C., Hua, W., & Huang, J. C. (2015). A cross-cultural examination of subordinates' perceptions of and reactions to abusive supervision. *Journal of Organizational Behavior*, 36(5), 720-745.

Vroom, V. H. (1964). *Work and motivation,* Wiley, New York.

Walker, L. (1979). *The battered woman.* Harper & Row, New York.

Wang, C. H., & McChamp, M. (2019). Looking at both sides of leader and follower political skill on work outcomes: the mediating role of job satisfaction. *Economic research-Ekonomska istraživanja*, 32(1), 824-849.

Wang, M. Z., & Hall, J. A. (2019). Political skill and outcomes in social life. *Personality and Individual Differences*, 149, 192-199.

Wang, R., Jiang, J., Yang, L., & Shing Chan, D. K. (2016). Chinese employees' psychological responses to abusive supervisors: The roles of gender and self-esteem. *Psychological Reports*, 118(3), 810-828.

Wang, W., Wang, Y., Zhang, Y., & Ma, J. (2020). Spillover of workplace IT satisfaction onto job satisfaction: The roles of job fit and professional fit. *International Journal of Information Management*, 50, 341-352.

Wang, W., Mao, J., Wu, W., & Liu, J. (2012). Abusive supervision and workplace deviance: The mediating role of interactional justice and the moderating role of power distance. *Asia Pacific Journal of Human Resources*, 50(1), 43-60.

Watkins, T., Fehr, R., & He, W. (2019). Whatever it takes: Leaders' perceptions of abusive supervision instrumentality. *The Leadership Quarterly*, 30(2), 260-272.

Weale, V. P., Wells, Y. D., & Oakman, J. (2019). The work-life interface: a critical factor between work stressors and job satisfaction. *Personnel Review*, 48(4), 880-897

Weiss, H. M. (2002). Introductory comments: Antecedents of emotional experiences at work. *Motivation and Emotion*, 26(1), 1-2.

Weiss, H. M., & Cropanzano, R. (1996). Affective events theory: A theoretical discussion of the structure, causes and consequences of affective experiences at work.

Weiss, H. M., & Cropanzano, R. (1996). Affective Events Theory: A theoretical discussion of the structure, causes and consequences of affective experiences at work. In B. M. Staw & L. L. Cummings (Eds.), *Research in organizational behavior: An Annual Series of Analytical Essays and Critical Reviews*, 18, 1-74. Elsevier Science/JAI Press, Greenwich.

Whitman, M. V., Halbesleben, J. R., & Shanine, K. K. (2013). Psychological entitlement and abusive supervision: Political skill as a self-regulatory mechanism. *Health Care Management Review*, 38(3), 248-257.

Williams, L. J., & Hazer, J. T. (1986). Antecedents and consequences of satisfaction and commitment in turnover models: A reanalysis using latent variable structural equation methods. *Journal of Applied Psychology*, 71(2), 219-31.

Wolfe, D. A. (1987). *Child abuse: Implications for child development and psychopathology*. Beverly Hills, CA: Sage.

Wright, T. A., & Bonett, D. G. (2007). Job satisfaction and psychological well-being as nonadditive predictors of workplace turnover. Journal of Management, 33(2), 141-160.

Wright, T. A., & Bonett, D. G. (1992). The effect of turnover on work satisfaction and mental health: Support for a situational perspective. *Journal of Organizational Behavior*, 13(6), 603-615.

Wu, T. Y., & Hu, C. (2009). Abusive supervision and employee emotional exhaustion: Dispositional antecedents and boundaries. *Group & Organization Management*, 34(2), 143-169.

Yam, K. C., Fehr, R., Keng-Highberger, F. T., Klotz, A. C., & Reynolds, S. J. (2016). Out of control: A self-control perspective on the link between surface acting and abusive supervision. *Journal of Applied Psychology*, 101(2), 292-301

Yousaf, A., Sanders, K., & Shipton, H. (2013). Proactive and politically skilled professionals: What is the relationship with affective occupational commitment? *Asia Pacific Journal of Management*, 30(1), 211-230.

Yüksel, A. (2017). A critique of "Response Bias" in the tourism, travel and hospitality research. *Tourism Management*, 59, 376-384.

Zhang, Y., & Bednall, T. C. (2016). Antecedents of abusive supervision: A meta-analytic review. *Journal of Business Ethics*, 139(3), 455-471.

Zhang, Y., Liu, X., Xu, S., Yang, L. Q., & Bednall, T. C. (2019). Why abusive supervision impacts employee OCB and CWB: A meta-analytic review of competing mediating mechanisms. *Journal of Management*, 45(6), 2474-2497.

Zhao, H., Peng, Z., & Sheard, G. (2013). Workplace ostracism and hospitality employees' counterproductive work behaviors: The joint moderating effects of proactive personality and political skill. *International Journal of Hospitality Management*, 33, 219-227.

Zhao, X., Hwang, B. G., & Lim, J. (2020). Job satisfaction of project managers in green construction projects: Constituents, barriers, and improvement strategies. *Journal of Cleaner Production, 246*, 118968.

Zhou, Z. E., Yang, L. Q., & Spector, P. E. (2015). Political skill: A proactive inhibitor of workplace aggression exposure and an active buffer of the aggression-strain relationship. *Journal of Occupational Health Psychology, 20*(4), 405-419.

Appendix

Questionnaires

<table>
<tr><td>Assignmqane Code:
Name:</td><td>Form B-I</td></tr>
</table>

SUBORDINATE'S SURVEY

<u>NOTE</u>
- Please keep this form confidential and do not show this to anyone.
- The anonymity of the responses is assured and the information being collected under this study shall remain confidential.

Below are a series of statements with which you may either agree or disagree. For each statement, please indicate the degree of your agreement/disagreement by selecting the appropriate number and the way you feel regarding your supervisor.	I cannot remember him/her ever using this behavior with me 1	He/she very seldom uses this behavior with me 2	He/she occasion-ally uses this behavior with me 3	He/she uses this behavior moderately often with me 4	He/she uses this behavior very often with me 5
1. My boss ridicules me.	1	2	3	4	5
2. My boss tells me my thoughts or feelings are stupid.	1	2	3	4	5
3. My boss gives me the silent treatment.	1	2	3	4	5
4. My boss puts me down in front of others.	1	2	3	4	5
5. My boss invades my privacy.	1	2	3	4	5
6. My boss reminds me of my past mistakes and failures.	1	2	3	4	5
7. My boss doesn't give me credit for jobs requiring a lot of effort.	1	2	3	4	5
8. My boss blames me to save himself/herself embarrassment.	1	2	3	4	5
9. My boss breaks promises he/she makes.	1	2	3	4	5
10. My boss expresses anger at me when he/she is mad for an-other reason.	1	2	3	4	5
11. My boss makes negative comments about me to others.	1	2	3	4	5
12. My boss is rude to me.	1	2	3	4	5
13. My boss does not allow me to interact with my coworkers.	1	2	3	4	5
14. My boss tells me I am incompetent.	1	2	3	4	5
15. My boss lies to me.	1	2	3	4	5

Please Rate the Following Statements about the work environment in your organization.	Strongly disagree 1	Disagree 2	Neutral 3	Agree 4	Strongly agree 5
1. One group always gets their way.	1	2	3	4	5
2. There are influential groups no one crosses.	1	2	3	4	5
3. Policy changes help only a few.	1	2	3	4	5
4. People build themselves up by tearing others down.	1	2	3	4	5
5. Favoritism not merit gets people ahead.	1	2	3	4	5
6. Employees don't speak up for fear of retaliation.	1	2	3	4	5
7. Promotion goes to top performers.	1	2	3	4	5
8. Rewards come to hard workers.	1	2	3	4	5
9. Employees are encouraged to speak out.	1	2	3	4	5
10. No place for yes men.	1	2	3	4	5
11. Pay and promotion policies are not politically applied.	1	2	3	4	5
12. Pay and promotion decisions are consistent with policies.	1	2	3	4	5

Please Rate the following statements	Strongly disagree 1	Disagree 2	Neutral 3	Agree 4	Strongly agree 5
1. I spend a lot of time and effort networking with others at work.	1	2	3	4	5
2. I can make most people feel comfortable and at ease around me.	1	2	3	4	5
3. I am able to communicate easily and effectively with others.	1	2	3	4	5
4. It is easy for me to develop good rapport with most people.	1	2	3	4	5
5. I understand people well.	1	2	3	4	5
6. I am good at building relationships with influential people at work.	1	2	3	4	5
7. I am particularly good at sensing the motivations and hidden agendas of others.	1	2	3	4	5
8. When communicating with others, I try to be genuine in what I say and do.	1	2	3	4	5
9. I have developed a large network of colleagues and associates at work whom I can call on for support when I really need to get things done.	1	2	3	4	5
10. At work, I know a lot of important people and am well connected.	1	2	3	4	5
11. I spend a lot of time and effort developing connections with others at work.	1	2	3	4	5
12. I am good at getting people to like me.	1	2	3	4	5
13. It is important that people believe I am sincere in what I say and do.	1	2	3	4	5

Please Rate the following statements		Strongly disagree 1	Disagree 2	Neutral 3	Agree 4	Strongly agree 5
14.	I try to show a genuine interest in other people.	1	2	3	4	5
15.	I am good at using my connections and networks to make things happen at work.	1	2	3	4	5
16.	I have good intuition or savvy about how to present myself to others.	1	2	3	4	5
17.	I always seem to instinctively know the right things to say or do to influence others.	1	2	3	4	5
18.	I pay close attention to people's facial expressions.	1	2	3	4	5

EMPLOYEES INFORMATION

Gender: ☐ Male ☐ Female

Age: ☐ Less than 25 years ☐ 25-30 years ☐ 31-34 years ☐ 35-40 years
☐ 41-44 years ☐ 45-50 years ☐ 51-54 years ☐ 55 years and above

Qualification: ☐ Intermediate ☐ Bachelors ☐ Masters ☐ Doctorate

Experience (current organization)
☐ Less than 5 years ☐ 6-10 years ☐ 11-15 years ☐ More than 15 years

Hierarchical Level:
☐ Entry level ☐ Middle level ☐ Senior level

Time spent under current supervisor:
☐ Less than a year ☐ 1 - 2 years ☐ 3 - 5 years ☐ 6 - 10 years
☐ More than 10 years

<table>
<tr><td>Assignmqane Code:

Name:</td><td>**Form B-II**</td></tr>
</table>

SUBORDINATE'S SURVEY

<u>**NOTE**</u>
- Please keep this form confidential and do not show this to anyone.
- The anonymity of the responses is assured and the information being collected under this study shall remain confidential.

Below are a series of statements with which you may either agree or disagree. For each statement, please indicate the degree of your agreement/disagreement by selecting the appropriate number and the way you feel regarding your supervisor.	Strongly Disagree 1	Disagree 2	Neutral 3	Agree 4	Strongly Agree 5
1. I often seriously think about quitting my organization.	1	2	3	4	5
2. I want to quit my organization.	1	2	3	4	5
3. I am actually planning to quit my organization.	1	2	3	4	5

Please Rate the Following Statements	Strongly Disagree 1	Disagree 2	Neutral 3	Agree 4	Strongly Agree 5
1. I find real enjoyment in my job.	1	2	3	4	5
2. I like my job better than the average person.	1	2	3	4	5
3. I am seldom bored with my job.	1	2	3	4	5
4. I would not consider taking another kind of job.	1	2	3	4	5
5. Most days I am enthusiastic about my job.	1	2	3	4	5
6. I feel fairly well satisfied with my job.	1	2	3	4	5

Form A-II

Employee Name for whom this form is filled: _______________________	**Assigned Code** (1, 2, 3, 4 or 5): _______________

<u>**NOTE**</u>
- To be filled by the supervisor.
- Please keep this form confidential and do not show this to anyone.
- The anonymity of the responses is assured and the information being collected under this study shall remain confidential.

Below are a series of statements with which you may either agree or disagree. For each statement, please indicate the degree of your agreement/disagreement by selecting the appropriate number.

Please rate your <u>SELECTED SUBORDINATE</u> on the following statements.	Un-acceptable 1	Below Average 2	Average 3	Above Average 4	Outstanding 5
1. Rate the overall level of performance that you observe for this subordinate.	1	2	3	4	5
	Very Ineffective 1	Ineffective 2	Neither effective nor ineffective 3	Effective 4	Very Effective 5
2. What is your personal view of this subordinate in terms of his or her overall effectiveness?	1	2	3	4	5
	Not Effectively At All 1	Somewhat Effectively 2	Neither Effectively Nor Ineffectively 3	Effectively 4	Very Effectively 5
3. Overall to what extent do you feel this subordinate has been effectively fulfilling his or her roles and responsibilities?	1	2	3	4	5
	Strongly Disagree 1	Disagree 2	Neither Agree Nor Disagree 3	Agree 4	Strongly Agree 5
4. My subordinate is superior to other subordinates that I've supervised before.	1	2	3	4	5

www.ingramcontent.com/pod-product-compliance
Lightning Source LLC
LaVergne TN
LVHW020913200726
843506LV00011B/1709